Behavioral Science & Policy
Volume 4 Issue 1 2018

ii
Editors' note
Steven Patierno & Sim B Sitkin

Features

1
Review
What is health equity?
Paula Braveman, Elaine Arkin, Tracy Orleans, Dwayne Proctor, Julia Acker, & Alonzo Plough

17
Proposal
Applying population health science principles to guide behavioral health policy setting
Catherine Ettman, Salma M. Abdalla, & Sandro Galea

27
Essay
The ubiquity of data & communication: A double-edged sword for disparities
Robert M. Califf

39
Report
Using pay-for-success financing for supportive housing interventions: Promise & challenges
Paula M. Lantz & Samantha Iovan

51
Essay
Improving the match between patients' needs & end-of-life care by increasing patient choice in Medicare
Donald H. Taylor, Jr.

62
Editorial policy

editors' note

Welcome to this special edition of *Behavioral Science & Policy*, dedicated to the complex issues surrounding health equity. This Spotlight Topic Forum was co-edited by Steven Patierno (Duke University), Ingrid Gould Ellen (New York University), and Todd T. Rogers (Harvard University) and draws on research presented at the daylong workshop Achieving Health Equity: The Impact of Housing, Employment, and Education on Health Disparities. This event was hosted by the Behavioral Science & Policy Association, Duke University, and Duke Health and sponsored by the Robert Wood Johnson Foundation.

The symposium drew attention to the interconnectedness of social, structural, and biological determinants of health and provided elegant examples of the ways that interwoven socioeconomic and geospatial factors drive health inequity.

As early as 1989, Dr. Samuel Broder, former director of the National Cancer Institute, acknowledged that "poverty is a carcinogen."[1] In 2003, the Institute of Medicine published *Unequal Treatment: Confronting Racial and Ethnic Disparities in Healthcare*, in which it stated, "A large body of published research reveals that racial and ethnic minorities experience a lower quality of health services, and are less likely to receive even routine medical procedures than are white Americans."[2] More than a decade later, policymakers continue to grapple with how to achieve health equity, but they now recognize that health inequity is driven by factors as diverse as housing, education, and employment and that achieving health equity will require multilevel interventions that address social and structural inequities in these domains.

This issue begins with an article in which Paula Braveman, Elaine Arkin, Tracy Orleans, Dwayne Proctor, Julia Acker, and Alonzo Plough provide a carefully crafted definition of *health equity*. This article, whose authors include scholars at the Robert Wood Johnson Foundation, is a detailed and thought-provoking follow-up to Braveman's 2014 commentary in *Public Health Reports*, "What Are Health Disparities and Health Equity? We Need to Be Clear."[3] In the article here, Braveman and her coauthors explain that because a "lack of shared understanding can be a serious obstacle to effective action," what is needed is a shared, unambiguous definition of health equity that can withstand social and political forces that seek to bend the definition to promote particular policies and practices. They propose a definition of health equity that is aimed at ensuring fair and just practices across all stakeholder sectors, is actionable, can be operationalized and measured, and accounts for social concerns. Achieving health equity will require reducing health disparities, both by improving the health of socially disadvantaged groups and by addressing social determinants of health disparities, including poverty and discrimination.

In the second article, Catherine Ettman, Salma M. Abdalla, and Sandro Galea propose a policy-impacting framework that allows for the assessment of a broad range of global, national, structural, and environmental health determinants and how these affect individual behaviors. They identify four principles that can serve as guides in the development of more effective health policies: (1) recognize that population health is not binary (sick versus not sick) but a continuum of symptoms from mild to severe; (2) focus on high-prevalence determinants that affect the most people rather than high-risk, low-prevalence behaviors of fewer individuals; (3) consider the trade-offs between health interventions that may be easy to carry out (but can unintentionally exacerbate disparities) and interventions that are more challenging to implement but may be more effective at mitigating disparities and have broader impacts; and (4) carry out quantitative return-on-investment analyses. In one example, they provide interesting insights into how the mental health of a large population, as a reflection of drug abuse rates, could be improved by reducing population-wide stressors that trigger depression, such as food and housing instability. In another example, they note that setting colorectal screening guidelines and encouraging people to be screened through their doctors increases screening rates overall but that screening rates can be differentially and negatively affected by differences in race, education, income, and access to a primary care provider. In contrast, when Delaware instituted an intervention that made screenings readily accessible to the state's whole population, the program eliminated the health disparity between Blacks and Whites, reduced colorectal cancer mortality in Blacks by 51%, and in the end proved to be cost-effective to the state.

The third article responds to the recognition that health policymakers, institutional and clinical decisionmakers, and patients today are drowning in data. This is not only because the volume of health-related data is exponentially expanding but also because our capacity to effectively use the plethora of data has lagged. Here, Robert M. Califf, former commissioner of the U.S. Food and Drug Administration and now vice chancellor for health data science at Duke University School of Medicine, considers the ways that the ubiquity of data and communication technology can be a double-edged sword for disparities. He notes that the computing power of a single smartphone exceeds the computing power of entire universities only a few years ago and that it is now possible to analyze health by collecting data on individuals and populations at the levels of neighborhoods and households based on how they interact with their digital devices. These data—biological, medical, social, and environmental—can either guide interventions to reduce disparities and help achieve health equity or be manipulated to exacerbate disparities. Califf identifies specific ways that addressing this challenge will require the collaborative and purposeful engagement of thinkers in medicine, law, technology, and ethics as well as of community members and policymakers—all of whom must work together to use health data to achieve health equity.

Our special issue ends with two granular proposed interventions. First, Paula M. Lantz and Samantha Iovan argue that safe and affordable housing is a critical social precondition for health and well-being and that a focus on housing-related issues can pay health-related dividends far beyond the investment. They focus on pay for success, a public–private partnership model, to finance housing interventions for low-income and vulnerable groups (such as the homeless, addicted, or formerly incarcerated), as a method of providing a variety of promising ways to enhance health equity and overall community health. They describe seven pay-for-success intervention models that have the potential for significant impact and thus merit more careful study. In the other article, Donald H. Taylor, Jr., tackles whether the United States could improve health equity by enabling patients to choose to forgo low-value health care in favor of high-value options that fit their needs better. Specifically, he makes the case for testing changes in Medicare that could give patients new evidence-based choices about their treatment that would allow them to receive more impactful and equitable care. He also provides provocative and intriguing ideas about the kinds of constructive and balanced choices patients would make if given information and options suited to optimizing individual and community health.

We hope you find this collection of Spotlight articles valuable. As always, we look forward to your feedback and suggestions for additional Spotlight Topic Forums for future issues of *Behavioral Science & Policy*.

references

1. American Cancer Society. (2011). *Special section: Cancer disparities and premature deaths*. Retrieved from https://www.cancer.org/content/dam/cancer-org/research/cancer-facts-and-statistics/annual-cancer-facts-and-figures/2011/special-section-cancer-disparities-and-premature-deaths-cancer-facts-and-figures-2011.pdf

2. Institute of Medicine. (2003). *Unequal treatment: Confronting racial and ethnic disparities in health care*. https://doi.org/10.17226/10260

3. Braveman, P. (2014). What are health disparities and health equity? We need to be clear. *Public Health Reports, 129*(1, Suppl. 2), 5–8. https://doi.org/10.1177/00333549141291S203references

Steven Patierno
Spotlight Editor

Sim B Sitkin
Founding Editor

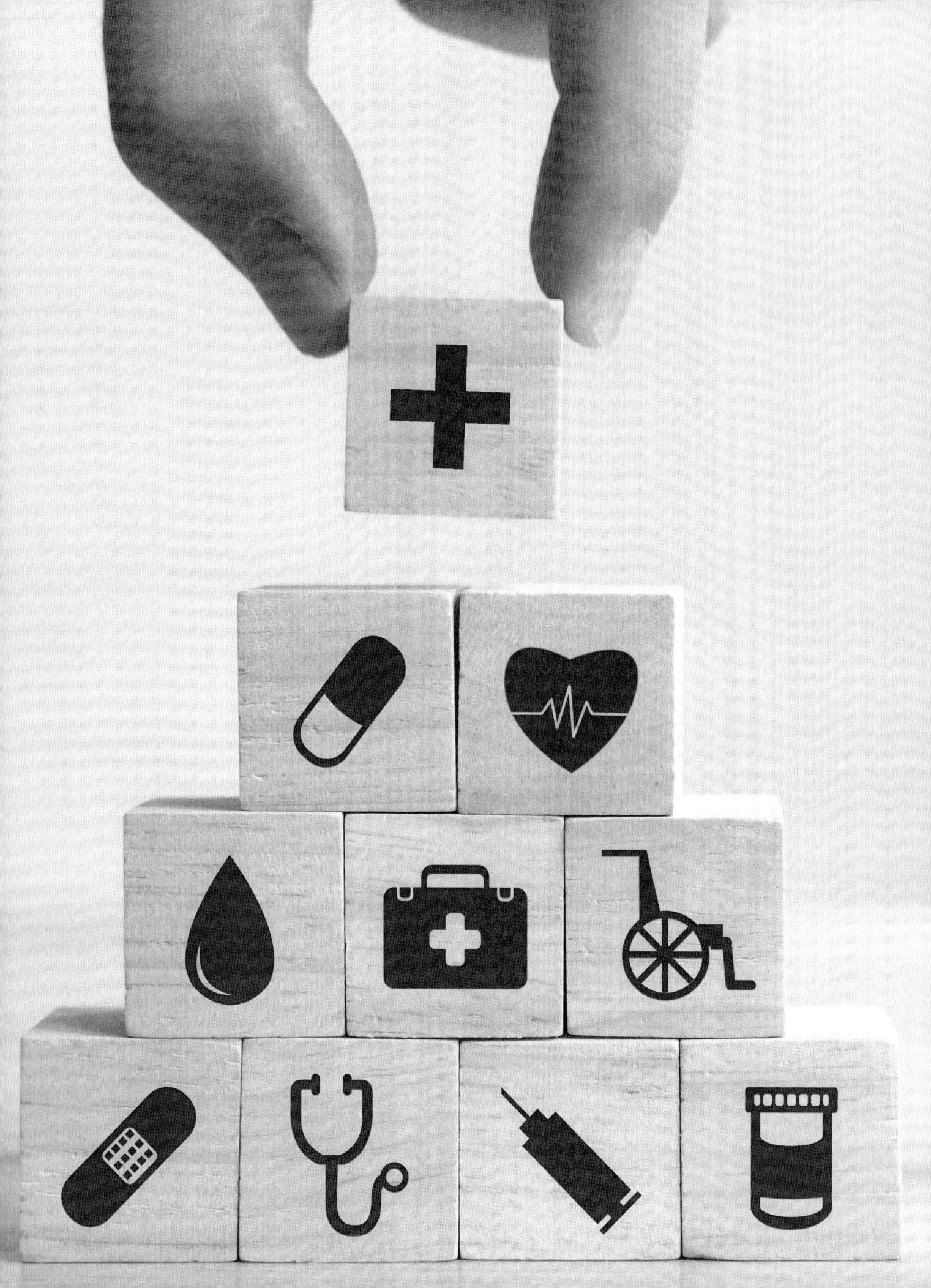

What is health equity?

Paula Braveman, Elaine Arkin, Tracy Orleans, Dwayne Proctor, Julia Acker, & Alonzo Plough

abstract

Policymakers and others concerned about public health often speak of the need to achieve health equity. Yet the term can mean different things to different people. For government, other organizations, and communities, lack of shared understanding can be a serious obstacle to effective action. This lack of understanding makes it difficult to agree on concrete goals and criteria for success and can lead to wasted efforts, with policies and practices that work at cross-purposes. This article provides a carefully constructed definition of *health equity* and discusses the definition's implications both for action and for assessing progress toward health equity.

Braveman, P., Arkin, E., Orleans, T., Proctor, D., Acker, J., & Plough, A. (2018). What is health equity? *Behavioral Science & Policy, 4*(1), 1–14.

Core Findings

What is the issue?
Different audiences tend to understand *health equity* differently. This can frustrate attempts to achieve desired health outcomes. Public health stakeholders need a common understanding of health equity in order to guide decision-making and resource allocation while maintaining respect for social groups of concern.

How can you act?
Selected recommendations include:
1) Simultaneously emphasizing the benefit of health equity measures to society at large and not only targeted groups
2) Constant monitoring of overall levels of health and health determinants within and across given populations

Who should take the lead?
Researchers, policymakers, and stakeholders in public health

Over the past two decades, the term *health equity* has been used with increasing frequency in public health practice and research. But definitions for this term vary widely. Some differ inconsequentially. Others, however, reflect deep divides in values and beliefs and can be used to justify and promote very different policies and practices. Clarity is particularly important when health equity is at stake because pursuing equity often involves a long uphill struggle against considerable resistance; in most cases, this struggle must strategically engage diverse stakeholders who have their own agendas. Under those circumstances, lack of clarity about the desired goal can put efforts to achieve health equity at risk of failure.

In this article, based on a report published by the Robert Wood Johnson Foundation,[1] we aim to stimulate discussion and promote greater consensus about the meaning of *health equity* and the implications this meaning has for action and research. In recommending a definition of the term, we are not aiming to have everyone use exactly the same words to define health equity. Rather, our goal is to identify crucial elements that can guide action in both public and private spheres. (The Robert Wood Johnson Foundation report, written by five of us—Braveman, Arkin, Orleans, Proctor, and Plough—includes content not in this article, such as examples of health equity efforts and resources for undertaking health equity initiatives.)

Throughout this article, the term *health* refers to health status or outcomes, distinct from *health care*, which is only one of many important influences on health. The term *social* encompasses economic, psychosocial, and other societal domains, although at times we refer separately to *social* and *economic* domains for emphasis. The Appendix provides definitions of many terms that are used in this article and often arise in discussions of health equity.

Criteria for a Definition

The following criteria were key to developing the definition of *health equity* that we share in this article. The definition had to:

- be conceptually and technically sound and consistent with current scientific knowledge;

- reflect the importance of fair and just practices across all sectors, not only the health care sector, because health is a product of conditions and actions occurring in virtually all social domains;

- be actionable and sufficiently unambiguous to substantively guide decisions about resource allocation priorities (some definitions may be meaningful or even inspiring to a segment of the public health community with experience in thinking about and pursuing health equity, but not specific or concrete enough to guide action, especially for a wider audience);

- be capable of being operationalized for the purpose of measurement, which is crucial in assessing whether interventions are working; and

- reflect respect for the social groups of concern.

The Definition

Application of the criteria led to a two-part definition. The first part is geared toward a broad, nontechnical audience; the second is needed to guide measurement and monitoring of how well efforts to improve health equity are working:

Health equity means that everyone has a fair and just opportunity to be as healthy as possible. Achieving this requires removing obstacles to health—such as poverty and discrimination and their consequences, which include powerlessness and lack of access to good jobs with fair pay; quality education, housing, and health care; and safe environments.

For the purposes of measurement, *health equity* means reducing and ultimately eliminating disparities in health and in the determinants of health that adversely affect excluded or marginalized groups.[2–5]

Different Definitions for Different Audiences

For many audiences or settings, the above definition will be too long or complex. The following are briefer and generally less complex alternatives, to be used with the understanding that they are backed up by the full definition:

An 8-second version for general audiences (defining *health equity* as a goal or outcome): **Health equity means that everyone has a fair and just opportunity to be as healthy as possible.**

Another 8-second version for general audiences (defining *health equity* as a process): **Health equity means removing social and economic obstacles to health, such as poverty and discrimination.**

A 15-second version for audiences concerned with measurement: **Health equity means reducing and ultimately eliminating disparities in health and in the determinants of health that adversely affect excluded or marginalized groups.**[2-5]

A 30-second definition for general audiences (consisting of the first part of the full definition above, minus the second part about measurement): **Health equity means that everyone has a fair and just opportunity to be as healthy as possible. Achieving this requires removing obstacles to health such as poverty and discrimination and their consequences, which include powerlessness and lack of access to good jobs with fair pay; quality education, housing, and health care; and safe environments.**

A 20-second definition to clarify the relationship between health equity and health disparities: **Health equity is the ethical and human rights principle that motivates people to eliminate disparities in health and in the determinants of health that adversely affect excluded or marginalized groups. Progress toward health equity is measured by reductions in health disparities.**

Explaining the Definition

Both *fairness* and *justice* are invoked in this definition to signify that achieving health equity in a population (for example, of a city, county, state, nation, or globally) involves not only meeting widely held standards of fairness, but also addressing broader ethical concerns and adhering to human rights laws and principles. Before people can achieve health equity, they must first be able to fully realize their human rights in all domains essential for health, dignity, and participation in society. They must be able to freely exercise not only civil and political rights—such as freedom of speech, assembly, and religion—but also social, economic, and cultural rights, including rights to education, decent living conditions, and freedom from avoidable obstacles to good health.[6]

A large and growing literature demonstrates that opportunities to be healthy depend on living and working conditions and other resources that vary across social groups.[7-13] The extent of a population's opportunities to be healthy, therefore, can be measured by assessing the social determinants of health—such as income, wealth,[14] education,[15,16] neighborhood characteristics,[17,18] or social inclusion[19]—that people experience across their lives. This concept acknowledges that individual responsibility is important, while recognizing that too many people lack access to the opportunities, conditions, and resources needed to make healthy choices and live the healthiest possible lives.[7,8,11,12] Societal action is needed to address these obstacles.

Health equity and health disparities are intimately related to each other. *Health equity* is the ethical and human rights principle that motivates people to eliminate *health disparities*, which are presumably avoidable differences in health or in its key determinants (such as good jobs with fair pay; quality education, housing, and health care; and safe environments) that adversely affect marginalized or excluded groups. Disparities in health and its key determinants are the metrics used to assess the extent

"Lack of political will does not justify considering a health disparity to be unavoidable"

of health equity and how it changes over time for different groups of people.

Being *as healthy as possible* refers to the highest level of health that could be within an individual's reach[5,20,21] if society makes adequate efforts to provide opportunities to achieve it. This notion acknowledges and takes into account the existence of some unavoidable variations in genetic endowment that may limit an individual's health potential. Even if someone has serious unavoidable biological disadvantages, the best health possible for people with those biological disadvantages could be achieved if societal efforts addressed that goal. For example, a person with a disability that makes her unable to walk can achieve better health if she has a properly designed wheelchair and if access to fixtures at home, on buses, and at work enable her to be more physically active, less isolated, and less dependent on others. Adequate societal efforts often depend on political will. Lack of political will does not justify considering a health disparity to be unavoidable. A health disparity should be considered avoidable if current scientific knowledge indicates that it could potentially and plausibly be reduced or eliminated if political will were present.

This definition implies that advancing health equity requires societal actions to increase opportunities to be as healthy as possible, particularly for the groups that have suffered avoidable ill health and encountered the greatest social obstacles to achieving optimal health. Workers in the health sector and much of the public will be motivated to take action for greater health equity by seeing evidence of significant health disparities—that is, presumably avoidable health differences on which excluded or marginalized groups fare worse than socially better-off groups. If one looks beneath the surface, however, and examines the results of extensive scientific research, it becomes apparent that most disparities in health are tenaciously rooted in profound inequities in the opportunities and resources that are needed to be healthier. The literature reveals that social inequities produce health inequities, which cannot be addressed effectively or in a lasting way without addressing their underlying causes.

A large body of knowledge indicates that pursuing health equity requires addressing equity not only in health care but also in a range of social determinants of health, particularly poverty,[10–12,14,22,23] discrimination,[11,19,24,25] and their consequences, including powerlessness and lack of access to a range of resources, services, and conditions needed for optimal health. Achieving health equity calls for removing obstacles and improving access to the conditions and resources known to strongly influence health, including good jobs with fair pay;[26] high-quality education,[15,16] housing,[27] and health care; and health-promoting physical and social environments,[17,28] particularly for those who lack access to these conditions and resources and who have worse health.[29,30] Although this strategy should ultimately improve health and well-being for everyone,[31] the systematic focus of action for equity should be on groups that have been excluded or marginalized.[30] The definition explicitly points to poverty and discrimination as underlying causes of health inequity. We wrote it this way to make the definition concrete and to reduce the ambiguity of more abstract and less specific definitions, which could be misused, perhaps unwittingly, to justify directing resources away from health equity.

Discrimination refers to adverse treatment of members of a social group based on prejudicial assumptions about the group as a whole. Discrimination may be based on any number of characteristics, such as race, ethnic group, religion, national origin, disability status, skin color, gender or gender identity, or sexual orientation. Discrimination or oppression is not necessarily conscious or intentional. Evidence has revealed that unconscious bias in interpersonal interactions is strong, widespread, and deeply rooted. Whatever the cause of the bias, it can take a heavy toll on the health of its victims. This conclusion is partly based on an understanding of the physiological mechanisms involved in responding to stress, particularly chronic stress.[24]

Discrimination does not occur only on the interpersonal level, though. It is often systemic, that is, built into institutional structures, policies, and practices—consider policing, bail, and sentencing practices that put people of color at a profoundly unfair disadvantage in the justice system; bank lending procedures that make it difficult or even impossible to build wealth in low-income, largely minority communities; and the underfunding of schools in racially segregated, poor communities, which denies children from these neighborhoods a good education and hence a good, decently paying job. These built-in features can have inequitable effects regardless of whether any individual consciously intends to discriminate. This systemic form of discrimination is also known as *structural* or *institutional discrimination*[32] or *systemic oppression*.

Racial segregation in housing in the United States is an example of systemic discrimination based on race or skin color. It is the product of deliberately discriminatory policies enacted in the past, including the Jim Crow laws that enforced segregation of dark-skinned people in the United States and practices affecting the sale and rental of housing.[33] Even though housing discrimination is no longer legal, many people of color continue to be relegated into neighborhoods that pose multiple challenges to health by exposing residents to a range of physical hazards (such as air pollution, other toxins, and unsafe housing conditions) and social hazards (such as concentrated poverty, absence of local employment, inadequate transportation to work and to better job prospects, poor schools, crime, an unhealthy food environment, hopelessness, and powerlessness). These places also lack the assets required for optimal health, such as good schools, optimism, clean air, green spaces, traffic patterns that minimize pedestrian danger, a feeling of safety, and the presence of many role models who set positive norms for healthy behaviors.[19]

Systemic discrimination has many other guises as well. Voter registration requirements in some states, such as the need to show a birth certificate, may discriminate against immigrants and homeless persons, who are less likely to have the necessary documentation even when they meet federal voter qualifications. People of limited financial means, meanwhile, face discrimination in the judicial system. A nonviolent, first-time criminal offender may qualify for a diversion program, which would allow the offender to avoid going to jail and to have the offense expunged from records, but only if the offender pays substantial fees. Thus, people with low incomes are far more likely to serve jail time and have criminal records than are more affluent people who have committed similar or worse offenses.[34] People of color are more likely than White people to be incarcerated for the same offenses, and a history of incarceration is a formidable obstacle to future employment, housing, and participation in society.[35]

Powerlessness is both an objective and a subjective phenomenon. Poverty and discrimination deprive people of economic and political power and make them less able to gain control of their lives and to access resources. Powerlessness becomes internalized when people perceive their inability to influence outcomes as a personal failure rather than a result of discrimination or systemic oppression.[36] Repeated or persistent experiences of powerlessness may lead to feelings of hopelessness and, subsequently, immobilization and an inability to assert one's rights or needs.

Excluded or *marginalized groups* are made up of people who have often suffered discrimination or been pushed to society's margins, with little or no access to society's health-promoting resources and key opportunities.[7,24] They suffer economic or social disadvantages or both,[37] and they lack privilege. Examples of historically disadvantaged groups who have been excluded or marginalized include—but are not limited to—people of color;[19] people living in poverty, particularly across generations;[22,38,39] religious minorities; people with physical or mental disabilities;[40,41] LGBTQ persons;[25,42] and women.[43]

Health Disparities
Avoidable differences in health or in its key determinants that adversely affect marginalized or excluded groups

Healthy as Possible
Highest level of health that could be within an individual's reach

Structural/ Institutional Discrimination
Systemic form of discrimination built into institutional structures, policies, and practices

> "A key feature of the definition of health equity is that it deliberately avoids the need to establish a causal role for any given factor in creating a health inequity"

A key feature of the definition of *health equity* is that it deliberately avoids the need to establish a causal role for any given factor in creating a health inequity. According to the definition, differences in health are inequitable if members of an excluded or marginalized group experience poor health that could plausibly have been avoided, given political will. It is important not to require proof of causation. The causes of some important health disparities—for example, racial disparities in premature birth—may be unknown or contested, making some people reluctant to call them inequities. These disparities should nevertheless be addressed in a health equity agenda because they put people who are part of a socially disadvantaged group at further disadvantage with respect to their health, regardless of the causes. If the disparities are known to be rooted in social inequities in access to the opportunities and resources needed for health, they can be referred to as *health inequities*. If the causes are not known, we prefer to emphasize the distinction by using a different term: *disparities* or *inequalities* (a term generally used outside the United States). Both *disparity* and *inequality* imply more than just a neutral difference, though: they suggest that there is something suspect about an observed difference and that discrimination may be involved.

This definition of *health equity* treats it as both a process[44] and an outcome, and it can be measured as either. The process is removing obstacles to health, particularly among those who have been excluded and marginalized. It also can be thought of as the process of reducing and ultimately eliminating disparities in health and health's determinants that adversely affect excluded or marginalized groups. Health equity also can be viewed as an outcome, namely, the ultimate goal of achieving fair and just opportunities to be healthy for everyone, or the elimination of health and health-determinant disparities that adversely affect disadvantaged groups.

Implications for Action

The definition presented here deliberately restricts what can be called an effort for health equity. Many actions may be worthwhile public health endeavors but not health equity efforts. For example, it could be important to address a health problem that primarily affects a high-income community; this, however, would not be a health equity endeavor, which prioritizes actions disproportionately benefiting those who have been socially disadvantaged. Similarly, an initiative to improve nutrition for the entire population of a state or nation might be worthwhile but would not be a health equity effort unless it devoted considerably more resources to improving nutrition among the disadvantaged. Likewise, an initiative to expand green spaces and recreational areas in solidly middle-class communities could be worthwhile from a public health perspective, but it, too, would not be a health equity initiative. Health equity should be one of the most central considerations driving policies that influence health, but not the only principle; other key principles that must also be considered are effectiveness, efficiency, overall population impact, and sustainability.

Policies, systems, and environmental improvements can prevent and reduce health inequities, but, in most cases, only if they explicitly and energetically focus on health equity and are well designed and implemented; otherwise, even well-meaning interventions may inadvertently widen health inequities. For example, in the early decades of anti-smoking efforts, messages about the health dangers of tobacco use were disseminated across entire populations. At some point, however, it became clear that the messages were primarily reaching White people of higher education levels. Smoking was declining among all groups, but the decline was far slower among people of color and less educated people. The understanding emerged that different messages and different methods for transmitting them were needed for

> "Equity is not the same as equality. Those with the greatest needs and fewest resources require more, not equal, effort and resources to equalize opportunities."

anti-smoking communications to be effective among less privileged groups.

Achieving health equity requires societal action to remove obstacles to health and increase opportunities for everyone to be healthier, while focusing particularly on those who have worse health, face more social obstacles to health, and have fewer resources to improve their health. In line with basic ethical concerns (such as for autonomy and respect for persons) and human rights principles (such as participation in society and in making decisions that affect one's well-being), advancing health equity requires engaging excluded or marginalized groups in planning and implementing the actions needed to achieve greater health equity. Equity is not the same as equality. Those with the greatest needs and fewest resources require more, not equal, effort and resources to equalize opportunities.

Although those who advocate for health equity will necessarily focus on the health needs of excluded or marginalized groups, they will garner support if they simultaneously call attention to the ways that achieving greater health equity will benefit all of society. For example, greater health equity should result in a more productive workforce and reduced spending on medical care for preventable conditions. Furthermore, advancing health equity requires achieving a more generally equitable society, and it has repeatedly been observed that overall health is better in more equal societies.[31] Some scholars have hypothesized that this pattern arises because more equal societies enjoy greater social cohesion and trust, which benefits everyone.[31]

Achieving health equity requires more than identifying and addressing overt discrimination. It also requires addressing unconscious and implicit bias and the discriminatory effects—intended and unintended—of systemic structures and policies created by historical injustices, even when conscious intent to discriminate is no longer present.

Ideally, a health equity effort would aim to improve the fundamental and structural causes of ill health, notably poverty and discrimination, as opposed to addressing only the consequences of those causes. It may not always be possible in the foreseeable future to alter the underlying causes, however. In those circumstances, it would be desirable, while alleviating suffering by addressing the consequences of the root problems, to also raise awareness (among the public, policymakers, and those most affected) of the need to address the root causes, thus paving the way for more effective action targeting the root causes in the future. For example, the problem of obesity is an important health equity issue, with a disproportionate burden of obesity among people of lower income and education and among people of color. A policymaker will probably not want to wait until all the upstream determinants of obesity and effective solutions for them are identified before putting in motion some downstream efforts—such as making it easier and more appealing for low-income people to engage in physical activity, increasing funding for physical education at schools, requiring that the caloric content of all foods be clearly noted, or taxing sugary sodas—that could have at least some impact in the short or intermediate term. But if the policymaker is aware of the more fundamental factors that are strongly suspected to be at the root of the problem—factors related to poverty and discrimination—a more long-term and ultimately more effective strategy addressing poverty and discrimination and why they often, but do not always, intersect can be pursued at the same time, with the understanding that the results may not be seen for quite a while.

Many groups of people are socially disadvantaged. To be effective, an organization may choose to focus on one or a select few disadvantaged groups. The depth and extent of disadvantage faced by a group (such as multiple versus single disadvantages),[20,23,38,45] as well as where maximal impact could be achieved, are legitimate considerations in choosing where to focus.[20,29,30] In addition, it should be noted that some individuals in an excluded or marginalized group may have escaped from some of the disadvantages experienced by most members of that group; these exceptions do not negate the fact that the group as a whole is disadvantaged in ways that can be measured.

Implications for Accountability: Measuring & Monitoring Health Equity

As the definition of *health equity* implies, measurement is not a luxury: it is crucial for documenting disparities and inequities and for motivating and informing efforts to eliminate them. Without measurement, there is no accountability for the effects of policies or programs.

A commitment to health equity requires constant monitoring of overall (average) levels of health and health determinants in a population, as well as routine comparisons of how more and less advantaged groups within that population are faring on relevant measures of health and health determinants. Overall levels of health are useful to know and are important, but they can hide large disparities among subgroups within a population. Measuring gaps in health and in opportunities for optimal health is important not only to document progress, but also to motivate action and identify the kinds of actions needed to achieve greater equity.

The definition of *health equity* calls for examining how well socially disadvantaged (excluded or marginalized) groups in a population fare on health and its determinants compared with advantaged or privileged groups.[46-48] Making this assessment requires having information on both (a) important measures of health and its determinants, including social determinants, and (b) the distribution of social advantage and disadvantage (inclusion versus exclusion or marginalization, or privilege versus lack of privilege); the information must identify which groups are most and least advantaged and define who should be compared. Because health equity is concerned with fairness and justice, gaps should be assessed using both measures that are absolute (such as differences between groups in the percentage of infants who survive until their first birthday) and measures that are relative (such as infants in Group X are twice as likely as infants in Group Y to die in their first year of life). The gaps between the advantaged and disadvantaged are closed by making concerted efforts to improve the health of excluded or marginalized groups, not by worsening the health of those who are better off.[49] For example, the relative gap between Black and White infants in the incidence of low birth weight narrowed during the period 1990–2010 in the United States; however, that trend did not represent the achievement of greater health equity, because it instead reflected an increase in the incidence of preterm birth among Whites rather than real improvement in that measure among Blacks.[50]

Disadvantaged groups should be compared with those who are most advantaged, not with the whole population (or the population average). Comparing the disadvantaged with the general population is not appropriate unless information on advantaged groups is unavailable, for a simple reason: when disadvantaged groups represent a sizable portion of the population—as is increasingly occurring in the United States—this approach compares the disadvantaged groups largely with themselves, thereby substantially underestimating the size of the gap between the disadvantaged and the advantaged.

Social advantage, privilege, inclusion, disadvantage, discrimination, exclusion, and marginalization can be measured in various ways, including by assessing indicators of wealth (such as income or accumulated financial assets),[14,51,52] influence,[7,36] and prestige or social acceptance (for example, educational attainment and representation in high executive, political, and professional positions).[53] They also can be measured by well-documented historical evidence of oppression or discrimination (such as slavery; displacement from ancestral lands; lynching and other hate crimes; denial of voting, marriage, and other rights; and discriminatory practices in housing, bank lending, and justice system).

Final Remarks

Health equity may seem to be a complex and elusive concept. The essence, however, consists of two basic elements: (a) reducing health disparities by improving the health of socially disadvantaged groups, and (b) addressing the social determinants of health disparities, including poverty and discrimination. It is important to be clear about what health equity is and what it is not; for example, it is a core aspect of public health, but it is not the only aspect that needs to be considered in public health actions. Clarity is important because efforts to move toward health equity will inevitably face powerful challenges. If those of us who wish to contribute to achieving greater health equity are not clear about where we are headed and why, we can be detoured from promising paths and perhaps even lose our way.

author affiliation

Braveman: University of California, San Francisco. Arkin: independent consultant. Orleans and Proctor: Robert Wood Johnson Foundation. Acker: University of California, San Francisco. Plough: Robert Wood Johnson Foundation. Corresponding author's e-mail: paula.braveman@ucsf.edu

author note

We thank the following individuals who provided comments on drafts of the report on which this article is based. The authors are solely responsible for the contents of this article:

Deborah Austin, ReachUp Inc.
Stephanie V. Boarden, PolicyLink
Karen Bouye, CDC Office of Minority Health and Health Equity
Renee B. Canady, Michigan Public Health Institute
Ana Diez Roux, Drexel University
Tyan P. Dominguez, University of Southern California
Mary Haan, University of California, San Francisco
Erin Hagan, Evidence for Action
Robert Hahn, Centers for Disease Control and Prevention
George Kaplan, University of Michigan (Emeritus)
Mildred Thompson, PolicyLink
Naima Wong Croal, National Collaborative for Health Equity

Appendix. Definitions of terms used in the article

discrimination

This is a broad term that includes but is not limited to **racism**. (Bold type indicates words defined in this appendix.) Prejudicial treatment, social exclusion, and marginalization have been based on a wide range of characteristics, including not only racial or ethnic group but also poverty, disability, religion, LGBTQ status, gender, and other characteristics.

ethnicity or ethnic group

These terms refer to belonging to a group of people who share a common culture (which may consist of beliefs, values, or practices, such as modes of dress, diet, or language) and usually a common ancestry in a particular region of the world. Some people use the term *ethnicity* or *ethnic group* to encompass both racial and ethnic groups, based on the recognition that race is fundamentally a social rather than biological construct. (See **race** or **racial group** below.)

health

Throughout the article, *health* refers to health status, that is, to physical and mental well-being, distinguished from health care, which is only one of many important influences on health.

health disparity and health inequality

These terms are synonyms; *disparity* is used more often in the United States, whereas other countries use *inequality*. Progress toward health equity is measured by assessing health disparities/inequalities. The concept of health equity is the underlying principle that motivates action to eliminate health disparities.

The terms *disparity* and *inequality* do not necessarily imply that social disadvantage is the cause of or a contributor to worse health, but they suggest that such a causal link should be considered. For over 25 years in the fields of public health and medicine, the terms *health disparity* and *health inequality* have referred to plausibly avoidable, systematic health differences adversely affecting socially or economically disadvantaged groups. This definition does not require establishing that the disparities/inequalities were caused by social disadvantage; it requires only observing worse health in socially or economically disadvantaged groups. Health disparities/inequalities are ethically concerning even if their causes are not clear, because they affect groups already at underlying economic or social disadvantage (due to poverty, discrimination, or both) and they indicate that these socially disadvantaged groups are further disadvantaged by having ill health on top of social disadvantage; this double whammy seems especially unfair because good health often is needed to escape social disadvantage.

It may seem reasonable to use the term *disparities* or *inequalities* to refer to only descriptive or mathematical differences without implying any judgment about whether they suggest cause for moral or ethical concern. However, social movements in the United States and other countries for nearly 30 years have treated these terms as indicating differences that are worrisome from ethical and human rights perspectives (although the groups of concern are not always the same). In the United States, health disparities have often referred to racial or ethnic differences in health, whereas in Europe and other regions, health inequalities have generally referred to health differences among people of different socioeconomic means. In theory, one might want to bring the definitions into alignment to simplify discussions of how to achieve health equity. But legislation and policies have been written based on the existing understandings of the terms, so redefinitions might have unintended consequences that could unwittingly threaten the achievements and momentum gained over decades. For example, some have proposed using the term *disparity* only to mean a difference, without any implication regarding whether the difference is morally suspect, and using the term *inequity* for racial or socioeconomic differences in health. If that change were made, then the resources now directed to national, state, and local efforts to reduce health disparities could be used for virtually any health improvement effort, including efforts focused on privileged groups. Furthermore, indiscriminately calling any racial or socioeconomic difference in health unfair (inequitable) would be unwise from a communications perspective, because there are some health differences whose etiology we do not know; the term *health disparity* is convenient to use for these differences, signaling reason for concern but not necessarily proof of a **health inequity**.

Health disparity and *health inequality* are broad terms that include **health inequity** and signify more than just difference or variation: they signify a health difference that raises moral or ethical concerns. These terms are very useful in identifying problematic areas (that is, an avoidable health difference that puts a socially disadvantaged group at further disadvantage on health) and being measurable, but they do not necessarily imply definitive knowledge of the causes.

health equity

This phrase means that everyone has a fair and just opportunity to be as healthy as possible. Achieving health equity requires removing obstacles to health such as poverty, discrimination, and their consequences, which include powerlessness and lack of access to good jobs with fair pay; quality education, housing, and health care; and safe environments.

For the purposes of measurement, *health equity* means reducing and ultimately eliminating disparities in health and health determinants that adversely affect excluded or marginalized groups.

Health equity is the ethical and human rights principle motivating efforts to eliminate health disparities; health disparities are the metric for assessing progress toward health equity.

health inequity

A health inequity is a particular kind of **health disparity**, one that is a cause for concern in that it is potentially a reflection of injustice. Views of what constitutes adequate evidence of a health inequity can differ. Some will argue that to call a disparity an inequity, one must know its causes and demonstrate that they are unjust. Others would maintain that regardless of the causes of a health disparity, it is unjust not to take concerted action to eliminate it; failure to act is unjust because the situation puts an already socially disadvantaged group at further disadvantage on health, and good health is often needed to escape social disadvantage. Where there is reasonable (but not necessarily definitive) evidence that underlying inequities in opportunities and resources to be healthier have produced a health disparity, that disparity can be called a *health inequity*; it needs to be addressed through efforts to eliminate inequities in the opportunities and resources required for good health. *Inequity* is a powerful word; its power may be diminished if it is used carelessly, exposing health equity efforts to potentially harmful challenges. It should be used thoughtfully.

opportunity

This means access to goods, services, and the benefits of participating in society. Financial barriers and geographic distance are not the only obstacles to access; others can include past discrimination, fear, mistrust, and lack of awareness, as well as transportation difficulties and family caregiving responsibilities. Measuring the real (or realized) access to opportunities that different social groups have requires not just measuring their potential access[54] but also assessing which groups actually have the relevant goods, services, and benefits. Because of past and ongoing racial discrimination in housing, lending, and hiring policies and practices, there is great variation in the quality of the places where people of different racial or ethnic groups live, work, learn, and play; these differences in quality often affect the opportunities groups have to be as healthy as possible.

race or racial group

This generally refers to a group of people who share a common ancestry from a particular region of the globe. Common ancestry is often accompanied by superficial secondary physical characteristics such as skin color, facial features, and hair texture. Given the extensive racial mixing that has occurred historically, these superficial differences in physical appearance are highly unlikely to be associated with fundamental, widespread, underlying differences in biology. This low probability of an association does not rule out the possibility that some highly specific genetic differences associated with ancestry could affect susceptibility to particular diseases (for example, sickle cell anemia, other hemoglobinopathies, or Tay-Sachs disease) or responsiveness to treatments. These highly specific differences, however, are not fundamental and do not define biologically distinct racial groups; they generally occur in multiple racial groups at different frequencies. The primary drivers of health inequities are differences in social and economic opportunities to be healthier. Scientists, including geneticists, concur that race is primarily a social—not a biological—construct.[55–57]

racism
This term refers to prejudicial treatment based on racial or ethnic group and the societal structures or institutions that systemically perpetuate this unfair treatment. Racism can be expressed on interpersonal, systemic, and internalized levels.[32]

Interpersonal racism is race-based unfair treatment of a person or group by individuals. Examples include hate crimes; name-calling; or the denial of a job, promotion, equal pay, or access to renting or buying a home on the basis of race.

Structural or *institutional racism* (also known as *systemic racism*) is race-based unfair treatment built into policies, laws, and practices. It often is rooted in intentional discrimination that occurred historically, but it can exert its effects even when no individual currently intends to discriminate. Racial residential segregation is an excellent example: it has steered people of color into residential areas where opportunities to be healthier and to escape poverty are limited.

Internalized racism occurs when victims of racism adopt (perhaps unconsciously) race-based prejudicial attitudes toward themselves and their racial or ethnic group, resulting in a loss of self-esteem and potentially in prejudicial treatment of members of their own racial or ethnic group.

social
Unless specified otherwise, this term encompasses (but is not limited to) economic, psychosocial, and other societal domains. In this article, at times *economic* is specified in addition to *social*, for clarity.

social determinants of health
These are nonmedical factors that influence health, such as employment, income, housing, transportation, child care, education, discrimination, and the quality of the places where people live, work, learn, and play. *Social* refers broadly to society—that is, people, their actions, and relationships. Social determinants are social in the sense that they are shaped by social policies. The World Health Organization Commission on the Social Determinants of Health[7] chose to include medical care (the services provided by trained medical or health personnel, such as doctors, nurses, therapists, pharmacists, and their support staff) among the social determinants, presumably because the provision of medical care—including access to it and its quality—is under the control of social policy. Generally, however, and in this article, the term *social determinants* refers to factors outside of medical care that influence health.

social exclusion or marginalization
This term refers to barring or deterring particular social groups—for example, on the basis of skin color, national origin, religion, wealth, disability, sexual orientation, gender identity, or gender—from full participation in society and from sharing the benefit of participation. Socially excluded or marginalized groups have less power and prestige and, generally, less wealth. Because they lack those basic resources, the places where they are able to live often are characterized by health-damaging conditions or conditions that fail to promote health, such as pollution, lack of access to jobs and services, and inadequate schools.

structural racism
See **racism**.

references

1. Braveman, P., Arkin, E., Orleans, T., Proctor, D., & Plough, A. (2017). *What is health equity? And what difference does a definition make?* Retrieved from Robert Wood Johnson Foundation website: https://www.rwjf.org/content/dam/farm/reports/issue_briefs/2017/rwjf437393

2. United States Department of Health and Human Services, Office of Disease Prevention and Health Promotion. (2018). Disparities. Retrieved from http://www.healthypeople.gov/2020/about/foundation-health-measures/Disparities

3. Braveman, P. A., Kumanyika, S., Fielding, J., LaVeist, T., Borrell, L. N., Manderscheid, R., & Troutman, A. (2011). Health disparities and health equity: The issue is justice. *American Journal of Public Health, 101*(S1), S149–S155.

4. United States Department of Health and Human Services, Office of Minority Health, National Partnership for Action to End Health Disparities. (2010). *Toolkit for community action*. Retrieved from http://www.minorityhealth.hhs.gov/npa

5. Braveman, P. (2006). Health disparities and health equity: Concepts and measurement. *Annual Review of Public Health, 27*, 167–194.

6. Braveman, P., & Gruskin, S. (2003). Poverty, equity, human rights and health. *Bulletin of the World Health Organization, 81*, 539–545.

7. World Health Organization Commission on the Social Determinants of Health. (2008). *Closing the gap in a generation: Health equity through action on the social determinants of health.* Geneva, Switzerland: World Health Organization.

8. Berkman, L. F., Kawachi, I., & Glymour, M. (2014). *Social epidemiology* (2nd ed.). New York, NY: Oxford University Press.

9. Marmot, M. (2015). The health gap: The challenge of an unequal world. *The Lancet, 386*, 2442–2444.

10. Marmot, M., Friel, S., Bell, R., Houweling, T. A., Taylor, S., & Commission on Social Determinants of Health. (2008). Closing the gap in a generation: Health equity through action on the social determinants of health. *The Lancet, 372*, 1661–1669.

11. Braveman, P., Egerter, S., & Williams, D. R. (2011). The social determinants of health: Coming of age. *Annual Review of Public Health, 32*, 381–398.

12. Adler, N. E., & Stewart, J. (2010). Preface to the biology of disadvantage: Socioeconomic status and health. In N. E. Adler & J. Stewart (Eds.), *Annals of the New York Academy of Sciences: Vol. 1186. The biology of disadvantage: Socioeconomic status and health* (pp. 1–4). New York, NY: New York Academy of Sciences.

13. Norman, D., Kennedy, B., & Kawachi, I. (1999). Why justice is good for our health: The social determinants of health inequalities. *Daedalus, 128*(4), 215–251.

14. Isaacs, S. L., & Schroeder, S. A. (2004). Class: The ignored determinant of the nation's health. *The New England Journal of Medicine, 351*, 1137–1142.

15. Cutler, D. M., & Lleras-Muney, A. (2006). *Education and health: Evaluating theories and evidence* (NBER Working Paper No. 12352). Cambridge, MA: National Bureau of Economic Research.

16. Egerter, S., Braveman, P., Sadegh-Nobari, T., Grossman-Kahn, R., & Dekker, M. (2011). *Education matters for health*. Princeton, NJ: Robert Wood Johnson Foundation.

17. Roux, A. V. D., & Mair, C. (2010). Neighborhoods and health. In N. E. Adler & J. Stewert (Eds.), *Annals of the New York Academy of Sciences: Vol. 1186. The biology of disadvantage: Socioeconomic status and health* (pp. 125–145). New York, NY: New York Academy of Sciences.

18. Acevedo-Garcia, D., Osypuk, T. L., McArdle, N., & Williams, D. R. (2008). Toward a policy-relevant analysis of geographic and racial/ethnic disparities in child health. *Health Affairs, 27*, 321–333.

19. Williams, D. R., & Mohammed, S. A. (2013). Racism and health I: Pathways and scientific evidence. *American Behavioral Scientist, 57*, 1152–1173.

20. Whitehead, M. (1991). The concepts and principles of equity and health. *Health Promotion International, 6*, 217–228.

21. Braveman, P., & Gruskin, S. (2003). Defining equity in health. *Journal of Epidemiology & Community Health, 57*, 254–258.

22. Wagmiller, R. L., & Adelman, R. M. (2009). *Childhood and intergenerational poverty: The long-term consequences of growing up poor.* New York, NY: National Center for Children in Poverty.

23. Evans, G. W. (2004). The environment of childhood poverty. *American Psychologist, 59*, 77–92.

24. Williams, D. R., & Mohammed, S. A. (2009). Discrimination and racial disparities in health: Evidence and needed research. *Journal of Behavioral Medicine, 32*, 20–47.

25. Meyer, I. H., & Northridge, M. E. (Eds.). (2007). *The health of sexual minorities: Public health perspectives on lesbian, gay, bisexual and transgender populations.* New York, NY: Springer Nature.

26. Burgard, S. A., & Lin, K. Y. (2013). Bad jobs, bad health? How work and working conditions contribute to health disparities. *American Behavioral Scientist, 57*, 1105–1127.

27. Edmonds, A., Braveman, P., Arkin, E., & Jutte, D. (2015). *Making the case for linking community development and health*. Princeton, NJ: Robert Wood Johnson Foundation.

28. Gordon-Larsen, P., Nelson, M. C., Page, P., & Popkin, B. M. (2006). Inequality in the built environment underlies key health disparities in physical activity and obesity. *Pediatrics, 117*, 417–424.

29. Daniels, N., Kennedy, B. P., & Kawachi, I. (2000, February 1). Justice is good for our health. *Boston Review.* Retrieved from http://www.bostonreview.net/forum/norman-daniels-bruce-kennedy-ichiro-kawachi-justice-good-our-health

30. Rawls, J. (1971). *A theory of justice.* Cambridge, MA: Belknap Press.

31. Pickett, K. E., & Wilkinson, R. G. (2015). Income inequality and health: A causal review. *Social Science & Medicine, 128*, 316–326.

32. Jones, C. P. (2000). Levels of racism: Theoretic framework and a gardener's tale. *American Journal of Public Health, 90*, 1212–1215.

33. Rothstein, R. (2017). *The color of law: A forgotten history of how our government segregated America.* New York, NY: Liveright.

34. Looney, A., & Turner, N. (2018). *Work and opportunity before and after incarceration.* Washington, DC: Brookings Institution.

35. Wildeman, C., & Wang, E. A. (2017). Mass incarceration, public health, and widening inequality in the USA. *The Lancet, 389*, 1464–1474.

36. Wallerstein, N. (1992). Powerlessness, empowerment, and health: Implications for health promotion programs. *American Journal of Health Promotion, 6*, 197–205.

37. United Nations General Assembly. (1966). *International covenant on economic, social and cultural rights.* Retrieved from http://www.ohchr.org/EN/ProfessionalInterest/Pages/CESCR.aspx

38. Reeves, R., Rodrigue, E., & Kneebone, E. (2016). *Five evils: Multidimensional poverty and race in America.* Washington, DC: Brookings Institution.

39. Cheng, T. L., Johnson, S. B., & Goodman, E. (2016). Breaking the intergenerational cycle of disadvantage: The three generation approach. *Pediatrics, 137,* 1–14.

40. United States Department of Health and Human Services, Office of Disease Prevention and Health Promotion. (2018). *Disability and health.* Retrieved from http://www.healthypeople.gov/2020/topics-objectives/topic/disability-and-health

41. World Health Organization. (2018). *Disabilities.* Retrieved from http://www.who.int/topics/disabilities/en/

42. Ward, B. W., Dahlhamer, J. M., Galinsky, A. M., & Joestl, S. S. (2014). *Sexual orientation and health among U.S. adults: National Health Interview Survey, 2013* (National Health Statistics Report No. 77). Retrieved from Centers for Disease Control and Prevention: https://www.cdc.gov/nchs/data/nhsr/nhsr077.pdf

43. Moss, N. E. (2002). Gender equity and socioeconomic inequality: A framework for the patterning of women's health. *Social Science & Medicine, 54,* 649–661.

44. Bluvas, E. (2016). Camara Jones inspires at the 9th Annual Clyburn Lecture with discussion on health disparities and racism. Retrieved from https://sc.edu/study/colleges_schools/public_health/about/news/2016/clyburn2016_recap.php

45. Ferraro, K. F., & Kelley-Moore, J. A. (2003). Cumulative disadvantage and health: Long-term consequences of obesity? *American Sociological Review, 68,* 707–729.

46. Harper, S., Lynch, J., Meersman, S. C., Breen, N., Davis, W. W., & Reichman, M. E. (2008). An overview of methods for monitoring social disparities in cancer with an example using trends in lung cancer incidence by area-socioeconomic position and race-ethnicity, 1992–2004. *American Journal of Epidemiology, 167,* 889–899.

47. Hosseinpoor, A. R., Bergen, N., Koller, T., Prasad, A., Schlotheuber, A., Valentine, N., . . . Vega, J. (2014). Equity-oriented monitoring in the context of universal health coverage. *PLoS Medicine, 11,* 1–9.

48. Mackenbach, J. P., & Kunst, A. E. (1997). Measuring the magnitude of socio-economic inequalities in health: An overview of available measures illustrated with two examples from Europe. *Social Science & Medicine, 44,* 757–771.

49. Whitehead, M., & Dahlgren, G. (2006). *Levelling up (part 1): A discussion paper on concepts and principles for tackling social inequities in health.* Copenhagen, Denmark: WHO Regional Office for Europe.

50. Martin, J. A., Hamilton, B. E., Ventura, S. J., Osterman, M. J. K., Wilson, E. C., & Matthews, T. J. (2012). Births: Final data for 2010. *National Vital Statistics Reports, 61*(1).

51. Pollack, C. E., Chideya, S., Cubbin, C., Williams, B., Dekker, M., & Braveman, P. (2007). Should health studies measure wealth? A systematic review. *American Journal of Preventive Medicine, 33,* 250–264.

52. Yeung, W. J., Linver, M. R., & Brooks-Gunn, J. (2002). How money matters for young children's development: Parental investment and family processes. *Child Development, 73,* 1861–1879.

53. Keyes, C. L. M. (1998). Social well-being. *Social Psychology Quarterly, 61*(2), 121–140.

54. Andersen, R., & Aday, L. A. (1978). Access to medical care in the US: Realized and potential. *Medical Care, 16,* 533–546.

55. Yudell, M., Roberts, D., DeSalle, R., & Tishkoff, S. (2016, February 5). Taking race out of human genetics. *Science, 351,* 564–565.

56. McCann-Mortimer, P., Augoustinos, M., & LeCouteur, A. (2004). 'Race' and the Human Genome Project: Constructions of scientific legitimacy. *Discourse & Society, 15,* 409–432.

57. Witherspoon, D. J., Wooding, S., Rogers, A. R., Marchani, E. E., Watkins, W. S., Batzer, M. A., & Jorde, L. B. (2007). Genetic similarities within and between human populations. *Genetics, 176,* 351–359.

proposal

Applying population health science principles to guide behavioral health policy setting

Catherine Ettman, Salma M. Abdalla, & Sandro Galea

abstract

Many behaviors, such as smoking and overeating, strongly affect a population's health. Further, social, physical, and economic contexts—for example, housing, transportation, education, and employment—shape health-related behaviors. To improve a population's health, policies must include actions that alter elements of these larger contexts. But the elements are vast and complex, and resources are limited. How can policymakers determine the right priorities to focus on? Building on the emerging field of population health science, we suggest four principles to guide priority setting: view population health as a continuum, focus on affecting ubiquitous influences on health, consider the trade-offs between efficiency and equity, and evaluate return on investment. This proposal offers a novel approach to setting policy for improving health behaviors.

Ettman, C., Abdalla, S. M., & Galea, S. (2018). Applying population health science principles to guide behavioral health policy setting. *Behavioral Science & Policy, 4*(1), 17–24.

Core Findings

What is the issue?
Policymakers need to implement formal principles from population health science into decisionmaking. These emphasize a broader understanding of health and equity while measuring the appropriate return on their investments. This will allow them to increase both the effectiveness and cost savings of public health care interventions.

How can you act?
Selected recommendations include:
1) Lowering obesity by increasing retail access to healthy food through tax breaks or subsidized loans
2) Providing preventative screening to populations composed of particularly vulnerable member groups
3) Measuring the savings from improvements in health care outcomes against the costs of direct and/or area-adjacent policy interventions

Who should take the lead?
Researchers, policymakers, and stakeholders in health care

Population health science researchers aim to understand the factors that affect the distribution of health-related features, such as cardiovascular disease, in a population so that policymakers can intervene and improve health on a societal scale.[1] This endeavor requires population health scholars to assess a broad range of health determinants, including global and national influences, urban structures and environments, individual behaviors, and the mechanisms that explain how each of these factors affects health.[2]

Consider, for instance, how the principles of population health science could help guide policymakers deciding on the right interventions for addressing the obesity epidemic. Obesity arises from molecular, individual, social network, and national causes. At the molecular level, genes shape people's vulnerability to obesity to some extent. Individual motivation dictates individual approaches to weight control, and friends in social networks affect individual decisions. National factors related to food availability—such as food policy and accessibility of safe areas for physical exercise—also determine whether people are likely to eat well and exercise. Therefore, any intervention to reduce obesity should rest on an understanding of the causes of obesity; their prevalence, complexity, and interactions; and how amendable any of these causes are to an intervention.

The challenges posed by a population health science approach to health policy are enormous and require enough insight into all the factors that affect health to be confident in the chosen interventions. If researchers and policymakers are to understand and intervene in factors ranging from national policy to individual behaviors, from urban planning to the molecular mechanisms that affect health, what should they focus on, and which of these factors are most likely to contribute to improved health in populations? Ultimately, to answer these questions, they must ask additional questions: What matters most?[3] What are the most important elements to study, and what are the best policy investments for improving population health?

There is no easy way to determine what matters most. A recent book on population health science has, however, proposed a formal set of nine principles that can guide scholarship in population health[4] and the setting of policy. Here we focus on four of these principles—the ones readily translatable to policy—and their application.

Principle 1: View Population Health as a Continuum

The first principle we explore holds that population health is best viewed as a continuum. This notion nudges thinking away from conceptualizing health as a binary (someone is sick or not sick) and toward recognizing that a population includes people with symptoms ranging from mild to severe, with only the people toward the severe end of the range meeting the criteria for a diagnosis. If health is framed as a continuum, behavioral health policies should focus on improving health in as broad a swath of the population as possible rather than focusing primarily on finding and treating people with a specific diagnosis.

The common approach to cholesterol testing in the United States is an example of misplaced emphasis. If a screening shows a person has high cholesterol, a health care provider is likely to worry about that person being at increased risk of cardiovascular disease. To counteract the high cholesterol and its possible effects, the health care provider is thus likely to prescribe cholesterol-lowering agents and recommend eating fewer saturated fats and exercising more. This practice, however, ignores the burden of poor health being borne by those whose cholesterol is certainly higher than the population's mean cholesterol but not over the cutoff that might suggest the need for intervention. These "borderliners" may get no such medicine or advice. A population health recommendation would rely on policy approaches that encourage everyone to eat healthy foods, not just those who already have high cholesterol, and would thus also protect the health of people who fall below the cutoff for what is considered a dangerous cholesterol level. Such advice, if followed, might prevent some from raising their cholesterol in the first place.

This emphasis on healthy eating rather than on cholesterol management would also help improve other aspects of population health that occur on a continuum. Policies to reduce the consumption of unhealthy food on a population scale could reduce the number of people who have or would otherwise come to have a high body mass index (BMI), which is a sign of being overweight or obese. Like having high cholesterol, being overweight or obese can increase the risk for heart disease. It also increases the risk of diabetes, which can contribute to heart attacks and other disorders.

How might policy achieve the more far-reaching goal of increasing healthy eating across a population? What people eat is driven in no small part by what is accessible, and there is a gap in healthy food accessibility in the United States. People living in low-income or minority-majority areas are more likely than those who live in middle-income areas to have access to overprocessed food, through inexpensive fast food outlets and convenience stores, and limited access to healthy food, which is usually available in large supermarkets. However, among participants in the U.S. food stamp program, easy access to supermarkets that provide fresh fruit and vegetables is associated with increased consumption of both.[5] One way to increase access to healthy food would be to encourage the establishment of retail stores and supermarkets that sell healthy foods in low-income neighborhoods, perhaps via subsidized loans or tax breaks.

In England, opening supermarkets in low-income neighborhoods led to a 60% increase in the consumption of fruit and vegetables among those who had poor diets before the intervention.[6] Opening stores in urban areas, where property is rarely cheap, may seem expensive, but here is why it makes economic sense: implementing interventions that shift a population's cholesterol or blood pressure levels in the right direction will lead to fewer people experiencing heart attacks or strokes in the future, reducing

"This notion nudges thinking away from conceptualizing health as a binary"

costs to both the health care system and the labor market. This approach was successful in both Finland and Japan.[7]

Another strategy to encourage a population to make better food choices would be to impose taxes on sugar-sweetened food and drinks, which play a role in increasing a population's BMI. Several countries and cities have implemented these taxes, which have reduced consumption of the taxed items. In Mexico, taxes on sugar-sweetened beverages reduced sales by 5% during the first year of their imposition and by almost 10% further during the second year. In Berkeley, California, a 25% tax increase on sugar-sweetened beverages resulted in a 21% reduction of sales in low-income neighborhoods merely four months after implementation.[8]

These examples suggest that policymakers who want to improve health behaviors related to food should shift their focus from trying to understand how to change people's specific dietary choices to thinking about how to ensure that healthy food is available to all and how to reduce the population's consumtion of unhealthy food. Although this advice may make intuitive sense, it has not typically been followed. To date, enormous effort has been expended on behavior modification efforts that can only plausibly benefit people who are at high risk for heart disease or other specific conditions rather than serving whole populations.

Principle 2: Focus on Affecting Ubiquitous Influences on Health

Health policymakers and health science researchers have historically been drawn to tackling factors that dramatically affect a person's health. They therefore tend to expend substantial energy on mitigating very dangerous behaviors, such as injecting heroin.[9] These efforts are important, and we do not mean to suggest that extraordinarily harmful behaviors should be ignored.

Yet, because extremely harmful behaviors are not particularly prevalent, behavioral policies aimed at them have a very small effect on overall population health. For example, in 2016, an estimated 948,000 people in the United States used heroin. By comparison, an estimated 3.7 million adults—nearly four times as many people—had a major depressive episode that same year. In 2016, roughly 35 million adults received mental health care, 37 times as many people as there are heroin users.[10] Although major depression is not as acutely threatening as heroin abuse, it is an important risk factor for a range of adverse consequences, including drug abuse[11] and suicide.[12] A population health approach would encourage policymakers to consider interventions that could influence the mental health of whole populations rather than that of people in one small, specific subgroup of the population. For instance, depression is influenced by stressors that may be ubiquitous in populations, such as food insecurity and housing instability.[13] Society may be better served, then, by instituting policies that reduce food insecurity and housing instability than by concentrating efforts solely on high-risk, low-prevalence behaviors that affect the health of only a few. Putting such policies in place will also help put a dent in the U.S. opioid epidemic.[14]

The city of Denver offers evidence for the wisdom of this approach. A supportive housing initiative for the chronically homeless there led to improvement in the overall health of participants. Specifically, 43% of those served by the initiative showed better mental health outcomes and a 15% reduction in substance use.[15] Another example is the Moving to Opportunity experiment in New York City, which relocated families living in public housing in high-poverty neighborhoods to low-poverty neighborhoods. Adult participants in the experiment showed a 20% reduction in depressive symptoms compared with participants in the control group.[16]

Once again, this principle can suggest a sea change in priority setting in behavioral science, from the factors that policymakers and researchers may be accustomed to focusing on—high-risk behaviors—to more common behavioral influences that may affect many more people on a daily basis.

Principle 3: Consider the Trade-Offs Between Efficiency & Equity

A danger of thinking in terms of populations is that it is easy to forget they consist of individuals of different races, ethnicities, genders, and socioeconomic classes and that these differences, as well as a range of other factors, can lead to variance in how these individuals behave and respond to different conditions. Helping one part of a population by implementing the easiest health policy intervention will certainly boost overall measures of health, but it may fail to assist other parts of the population, often those who are disadvantaged. To choose among potential interventions, policymakers therefore need to consider whether they value efficiency over health equity or vice versa.

The United States approach to colorectal cancer screening illustrates this trade-off. To increase screening rates, the U.S. Preventive Services Task Force developed national guidelines. The guidelines, which focused on reaching health care providers and on educational campaigns, led to an increase in screening rates in the United States from 38.2% in 2000 to 62.9% in 2015.[17] Yet follow-up studies consistently showed a gap in screening rates. One nationally representative analysis found that people with a primary health care provider (that is, someone they thought of as their doctor) were almost four times as likely to receive a screening test as were those without such a provider. The analysis also found that race, educational level, and income all contributed to the probability of undergoing a screening test. Those with at least one primary health care provider tended to be older, female, and non-Hispanic White; tended to have higher income, more education, and health insurance; and were most likely to receive up-to-date colorectal cancer screening.[18]

3.7M
Americans who had a major depressive episode in 2016

$147–$210 billion
Cost of the obesity epidemic per year in the United States

8.5 to 1
benefit : cost for colorectal cancer screening program that targeted uninsured persons

Informational campaigns that notify people who have stable health care providers about the availability of screenings will encourage those individuals to connect with their provider and arrange a screening. Overall screening rates will increase. But this approach is unlikely to do much for marginalized populations who do not have regular care providers, thereby widening gaps between health haves and health have-nots.

By contrast, screening programs that focus on narrowing health gaps can indeed reduce these gaps. To shrink racial disparities in disease incidence and mortality in Delaware, the state government created a screening program available to the entire population (that is, a population-based intervention). Further, the program offered treatment at no cost for uninsured individuals who screened positive for colorectal cancer. In addition to increasing the overall screening rate, the Delaware program reduced morality rates from colorectal cancer among African Americans by 51%, nearly eliminating the gap between them and Whites.[19] Although this program cost the state $1 million per year, as we note later, it was highly cost effective.

Massachusetts General Hospital Chelsea HealthCare Center, a community health center, adopted a different approach to colorectal cancer screening, reducing the screening gap between Latino patients and all patients visiting the center. The hospital provided outreach workers who matched patients both culturally and linguistically to help them navigate the health care system and tackle barriers to cancer care. Within four years, the program improved both the overall screening rates and health equity in vulnerable populations, especially when compared with the performance of other practices in the area.[20]

Similar trends have been seen with both cervical and breast cancer screenings. A review of screening programs in 22 European countries found smaller differences in screening rates between lower socioeconomic and higher socioeconomic groups in countries that provided national screening programs for their entire population, as compared with countries where screening is more dependent on an individual's ability to access the health care system.[21] Population-based approaches may, in the short run, be more difficult and costly to implement than education campaigns, but these European countries made a priority of improving health in disadvantaged groups.

"screening programs that focus on narrowing health gaps can indeed reduce these gaps"

The national colorectal cancer screening education program in the United States efficiently improved screening rates when the population is viewed as a whole but at the cost of increasing inequities within the population. Is this trade-off justifiable? This question is not a scientific issue but a values question, and it is one that can be answered only if policymakers are aware of the values they bring to their work. In some circumstances, they may consider a trade-off between efficiency and equity acceptable. For example, when an infectious disease epidemic is raging, achieving high rates of vaccination quickly is important, regardless of the cost or uneven distribution of services. At other times, making decisions without thought to the trade-offs and how to value them is indefensible. Conscious consideration of trade-offs between efficiency and equity should be front and center in behavioral science health policy discussions of both researchers and policymakers. There are no rules of thumb about what should be valued, but the very act of raising the notion that values dictate how people act can push policymakers to reckon with the trade-offs we are making implicitly, to the end of forcing us to be honest about why we choose to act in the way we do.

Principle 4: Evaluate Return on Investment

Prevention is the heart of population health thinking and public health practice. Most people

> "Supporting public transportation would also help address the obesity epidemic"

would prefer not being sick in the first place to being treated for illness. When policymakers are setting priorities, they should consider another compelling argument for favoring programs that could prevent disease: such policies can yield a good return on investment, in terms of both improved population health and cost savings. Policymakers who want to improve public health should assess programs' potential return on investment as they consider which ones to implement.

The Denver program supporting housing stability mentioned earlier offers a case in point: it led to the city achieving a net cost savings of $4,745 per participant by preventing unfavorable health outcomes.[16] The colorectal screening program in Delaware cost the state $1 million annually, but it led to $8.5 million in annual savings from reductions in costs related to colorectal cancer.[19]

A return-on-investment approach examines the yield on a particular policy intervention. Potential interventions can be evaluated by considering the extent to which any particular approach is likely to yield returns in health, whether that return is worth the financial and other costs of a particular effort, and, most practically, how one intervention compares with another on those features. Metrics to measure return on investment in population health can be described in terms of actual health benefits, cost benefits, or many other parameters. For example, one metric by which one can assess the success of a subsidized gym membership program is the number of sick days taken during a time period. (Society benefits from having healthier workers who miss fewer days of work.) In addition to occurrences of a specific health event during a time period and all-cause or disease-specific mortality, common metrics to measure return on investment include improvements in disability adjusted life years (DALYs) or quality adjusted life years (QALYs) gained through an intervention. Both measures assess the effects of interventions on years and quality of life, albeit in different ways.

Let's look at transportation investments for a fuller example of return-on-investment considerations. In a city of a million people, a 40% expansion of public transit systems delivers an annual health benefit worth more than $200 million.[22] This yield comes from spurring people to walk more and reducing pollution, among other benefits. This finding is a compelling argument for investing in transportation as a health policy.

Yet that is not the only argument for expanding public transportation. Supporting public transportation would also help address the obesity epidemic, which has real, crippling costs ranging from $147 to $210 billion per year in the United States.[23] Such an intervention can be a win–win for city planning, health system costs, and the health of populations alike.[24] The benefit of reducing obesity would extend even further, because of obesity's contribution to the burden of such chronic conditions as diabetes, heart disease, and cancer. Health care for people with multiple chronic conditions represented 71% of health care expenditures in the United States in 2010.[25] In 2012, the estimated costs of diagnosed cases of diabetes were $245 billion.[26] A 10% reduction in mortality due to heart disease, cancer, and diabetes in the United States would generate a return on investment of $10.9 trillion.[27] Viewed as a return-on-investment argument, investments in public transportation clearly have the potential to deliver enormous yields in population health.

Returns on early childhood education investments provide more support for this principle. One program showed, for example, that early childhood education provides a 5:1 return relative to costs, with positive outcomes taking the form of reductions in crime rates, child maltreatment, and teen pregnancy, as well as gains in academic achievement.[28] The Perry Preschool

Project, established in the 1960s, is also instructive. The school delivered high-quality education to 3- and 4-year-old African-American children living in poverty. Children attended daily educational sessions and received weekly home visits to involve their mothers in the educational process. Forty years later, 77% of those children had graduated from high school, compared with 60% of the children from the control group. Participants in the Perry Preschool Project were 20% more likely than those in the control group to earn more than $20,000 a year, and they had lower crime rates.[29] The effects of early education extended to providing both direct and indirect health benefits. Early education predicts higher education attainment, which, in turn, predicts a better ability to make health-related decisions as well as higher income levels. All of those factors ultimately play roles in determining the health of an individual.

Beyond providing clarity to policymakers directly concerned with improving population health, return-on-investment assessments for proposed recommendations can help sell those recommendations to leaders in the private sector, whose decisions inevitably influence how people behave and how healthy they are.

In Conclusion

Figuring out how best to enhance population health is a daunting undertaking, considering all the public health, social, and economic levers that can be pulled. The principles outlined in this article should help policymakers organize their thinking and establish policies and programs that will do the most good, maximally improving the health of the communities they serve.

author affiliation

Ettman: Boston University and Brown University. Abdalla and Galea: Boston University. Corresponding author's e-mail: sgalea@bu.edu.

references

1. Keyes, K. M., & Galea, S. (2016). Setting the agenda for a new discipline: Population health science. *American Journal of Public Health, 106*, 633–634.

2. Kaplan, R. M. (2004). Shared medical decision making: A new tool for preventive medicine. *American Journal of Preventive Medicine, 26*, 81–83.

3. Keyes, K., & Galea, S. (2015). What matters most: Quantifying an epidemiology of consequence. *Annals of Epidemiology, 25*, 305–311. https://doi.org/10.1016/j.annepidem.2015.01.016

4. Keyes, K. M., & Galea, S. (2016). *Population health science*. New York, NY: Oxford University Press.

5. Rose, D., & Richards, R. (2014). Food store access and household fruit and vegetable use among participants in the US food stamp program. *Public Health Nutrition, 7*, 1081–1088. https://doi.org/10.1079/PHN2004648

6. Wrigley, N., Warm, D., & Margetts, B. (2003). Deprivation, diet, and food-retail access: Findings from the Leeds 'food deserts' study. *Environment and Planning A: Economy and Space, 35*, 151–188. https://doi.org/10.1068/a35150

7. World Health Organization. (2002). *Chapter 6: Strengthening risk prevention policies*. Retrieved from http://www.who.int/whr/2002/en/Chapter6.pdf?ua=1

8. Sweet success: Will sugar taxes improve health? [Editorial]. (2017). *The Lancet Diabetes & Endocrinology, 5*, 235. Retrieved from https://doi.org/10.1016/S2213-8587(17)30070-0

9. Irwin, A., Jozaghi, E., Weir, B. W., Allen, S. T., Lindsay, A., & Sherman S. G. (2017). Mitigating the heroin crisis in Baltimore, MD, USA: A cost-benefit analysis of a hypothetical supervised injection facility. *Harm Reduction Journal, 14*, 1–14. https://doi.org/10.1186/s12954-017-0153-2

10. Center for Behavioral Health Statistics and Quality. (2016). *Key substance use and mental health indicators in the United States: Results from the 2015 National Survey on Drug Use and Health* (HHS Publication No. SMA 16-4984, NSDUH Series H-51). Retrieved from https://www.samhsa.gov/data/sites/default/files/NSDUH-FFR1-2015/NSDUH-FFR1-2015/NSDUH-FFR1-2015.pdf

11. Grant, B. F. (1995). Comorbidity between DSM–IV drug use disorders and major depression: Results of a national survey of adults. *Journal of Substance Abuse, 7*, 481–497. https://doi.org/10.1016/0899-3289(95)90017-9

12. Nock, M. K., Hwang, I., Sampson, N. A., & Kessler, R. C. (2010). Mental disorders, comorbidity and suicidal behavior: Results from the National Comorbidity Survey Replication. *Molecular Psychiatry, 15*, 868–876. https://doi.org/10.1038/mp.2009.29

13. Black, M. M., Quigg, A. M., Cook, J., Casey, P. H., Cutts, D. B., Chilton, M., . . . Frank, D. A. (2012). WIC participation and attenuation of stress-related child health risks of household food insecurity and caregiver depressive symptoms. *Archives of Pediatric Adolescent Medicine, 166*, 444–451. https://doi.org/10.1001/archpediatrics.2012.1

14. Abt Associates. (n.d.). *Opioid use disorder (OUD), housing instability, and housing options for recovery*. Retrieved from https://www.abtassociates.com/projects/opioid-use-disorder-oud-housing-instability-and-housing-options-for-recovery

15. Perlman, J., & Parvensky, J. (2006). *Cost benefit analysis and program outcomes report*. Retrieved from https://shnny.org/uploads/Supportive_Housing_in_Denver.pdf

16. Leventhal, T., & Brooks-Gunn, J. (2003). Moving to opportunity: An experimental study of neighborhood effects on mental health. *American Journal of Public Health, 93*, 1576–1582. https://doi.org/10.2105/AJPH.93.9.1576

17. National Cancer Institute. (2017). Colorectal cancer screening. Retrieved from https://progressreport.cancer.gov/detection/colorectal_cancer

18. Cardarelli, R., & Thomas, J. E. (2009). Having a personal health care provider and receipt of colorectal cancer testing. *Annals of Family Medicine, 7*, 5–10. https://doi.org/10.1370/afm.904

19. Verma, M., Sarfaty, M., Brooks, D., & Wender, R. C. (2015). Population-based programs for increasing colorectal cancer screening in the United States. *CA: A Cancer Journal for Clinicians, 65*, 496–510. https://doi.org/10.3322/caac.21295

20. Percac-Lima, S., López, L., Ashburner, J. M., Green, A. R., & Atlas, S. J. (2014). The longitudinal impact of patient navigation on equity in colorectal cancer screening in a large primary care network. *Cancer, 120*, 2025–2031. https://doi.org/10.1002/cncr.28682

21. Palència, L., Espelt, A., Rodríguez-Sanz, M., Puigpinós, R., Pons-Vigués, M., Pasarin, M. I., . . . Borrell, C. (2010). Socio-economic inequalities in breast and cervical cancer screening practices in Europe: Influence of the type of screening program. *International Journal of Epidemiology, 39*, 757–765. https://doi.org/10.1093/ije/dyq003

22. Litman, T. (2010). *Evaluating public transportation health benefits*. Retrieved from https://www.apta.com/resources/reportsandpublications/Documents/APTA_Health_Benefits_Litman.pdf

23. Strategies to Overcome and Prevent Obesity Alliance & The George Washington University School of Public Health & Health Services. (2017). *Fast facts: The cost of obesity* [Fact sheet]. Retrieved from http://stopobesityalliance.org/wp-content/themes/stopobesityalliance/pdfs/Fast%20Facts%20Cost%20of%20Obesity.pdf

24. Cawley, J., & Meyerhoefer, C. (2012). The medical care costs of obesity: An instrumental variables approach. *Journal of Health Economics, 31*, 219–230. https://doi.org/10.1016/j.jhealeco.2011.10.003

25. Gerteis, J., Izrael, D., Deitz, D., LeRoy, L., Ricciardi, R., Miller, T., & Basu, J. (2014). *Multiple chronic conditions chartbook: 2010 Medical Expenditure Panel Survey data*. Retrieved from https://www.ahrq.gov/sites/default/files/wysiwyg/professionals/prevention-chronic-care/decision/mcc/mccchartbook.pdf

26. American Diabetes Association. (2018). The cost of diabetes. Retrieved from http://www.diabetes.org/advocacy/news-events/cost-of-diabetes.html

27. Harvard School of Public Health. (2012). Infographic: The dollars and sense of chronic disease. Retrieved from https://www.hsph.harvard.edu/news/magazine/f12-infographic-chronic-disease/

28. Halfon, N., & Hochstein, M. (2002). Life course health development: An integrated framework for developing health, policy, and research. *The Milbank Quarterly, 80*, 433–479. https://doi.org/10.1111/1468-0009.00019

29. Schweinhart, L. J., Montie, J., Xiang, Z., Barnett, W. S., Belfield, C. R., & Nores, M. (2005). *Lifetime effects: The High/Scope Perry Preschool study through age 40* (Monographs of the High/Scope Educational Research Foundation, No. 14). Ypsilanti, MI: High/Scope Press.

The ubiquity of data & communication: A double-edged sword for disparities

Robert M. Califf

essay

abstract

The fourth industrial revolution, in which most information is stored in digital form, is characterized by connectivity and communication among people and groups via, for instance, cell phones and smart watches. The amount of information now generated about people's health-related activities is multiple log orders more voluminous and complex than the data currently captured in the electronic health record from patient interactions with clinicians. Despite the data's complexity, it is now possible for health care administrators, policymakers, and clinical researchers to develop—and then test—data-informed interventions that could reduce health disparities. For example, programs initiated by a county government and a major medical system have, respectively, improved asthma management and reduced lead exposure in their localities. Use of big data can be a double-edged sword, however. The technology that allows for high-end use of data also opens the way to increasing disparities, as could happen, for instance, if geospatial information were used to locate clinics in places that optimize profit rather than meet health needs. Efforts are underway to limit this risk.

Califf, R. M. (2018). The ubiquity of data & communication: A double-edged sword of disparities. *Behavioral Science & Policy, 4*(1), 27–37.

Core Findings

What is the issue?
The advent of the fourth industrial revolution has brought a wealth of new technologies and an exponential increase in information. This presents an unprecedented opportunity to address disparities in health care. New methods of data curation and analysis can lead to more effective interventions. But without societal involvement and participation in guiding new technology, health disparities are at risk of becoming more acute.

How can you act?
Selected recommendations include:
1) Developing a single standard for health care data pertinent to health outcomes
2) Using new technologies to provide useful information in a way that is tailored to the specific health needs of an individual, family, or population group

Who should take the lead?
Researchers, policymakers, and stakeholders in health care

For decades, it has been common knowledge that vast disparities in health outcomes and access to health care occur both in the United States and across the globe. Until recently, clinicians, health care administrators, policymakers, and clinical researchers have lacked timely access to the type and quantity of information that would enable interventions that might ameliorate disparities between individuals and populations. With the advent of the fourth industrial revolution,[1] that situation is quickly changing.

Whereas the third industrial revolution was marked by the introduction of digital technologies such as the Internet and personal computers, the fourth industrial revolution is characterized by the merging of biological, physical, and information sciences.[1] This fourth revolution has enormously expanded connectivity and communication among individuals and groups. For instance, today's cell phones reach almost everyone on the planet, regardless of income, education, and physical location, and they provide instant access to vast digital communication and information systems. Given the almost universal ability to connect to distributed cloud computing, the computing power accessible through a typical cell phone today exceeds the computational resources of entire universities or medical centers from just a few years ago.

New technologies for mapping and wayfinding illustrate the potential of the connectivity and communication that are hallmarks of the fourth revolution. Many drivers already rely on global positioning systems to help them navigate unfamiliar streets and highways, using information that is accessed, contextualized, and integrated in real time. Smart wayfinding apps provide a driver with current data about the driver's location, traffic and road conditions, upcoming businesses and landmarks, and reports from other drivers. This information helps drivers avoid accidents, potholes, and traffic jams. Drivers also receive predictions about the impact of interventions (such as the effect on driving time that taking a different route might have) to support their decisionmaking. Actual results of driving experiences are then fed back into the algorithms to improve them. Some key innovations relate to data fluidity—the capacity for data to flow easily and without undue friction among all the users who need it—and data latency—the speed at which data, once gathered, is available for analysis.

What if a similar approach were taken to human health care, including treatment and prevention? I argue that the ubiquity of data and its rapid communication provide previously unimaginable resources for understanding and addressing health disparities. One simple possibility is that home services could be better coordinated by systematically applying optimized transportation routing and scheduling of the kind now available with smartphone apps. Thus, a patient with uncontrolled diabetes living in an underresourced neighborhood would receive more frequent home visits from a nurse than a less ill person would.

Already, in Durham County, North Carolina, a data system connected to the Duke University Health System has contributed to a substantial improvement in locating children with elevated blood lead levels.[2] The Duke system created a map that estimates household lead exposure risk based on county tax assessor data, blood lead screening results from clinic visits, and census data. Stakeholders, including the Durham County Health Department and several community advocacy groups, have used this map to reach at-risk families.

Similarly, in Louisville, Kentucky, the public–private AIR Louisville consortium is helping local residents manage their asthma, a disorder that disproportionately affects Black children and people living below the poverty line.[3] Relying on electronic sensors in inhalers, the program provides feedback about triggers, adherence to treatment, and level of control to asthma patients, which has resulted in a 78% reduction in rescue inhaler use and a 48% improvement in the number of symptom-free days. After combining crowd-sourced data on inhaler use with environmental information, a government and community activist team crafted policy recommendations to lower the incidence of asthma attacks citywide, such as increasing the

> "Researchers and clinicians are now able to amass novel kinds of biological data, such as an individual's genetic code"

tree canopy (to reduce air pollution and urban heat), requiring that facilities with vulnerable populations (such as children and the elderly) be located at least 500 feet from roadways with high traffic and high emissions, and developing a community notification system that alerts asthma sufferers when high-risk conditions are about to occur.

Although this powerful technology can be harnessed to reduce health disparities, it may also exacerbate them.[4] For instance, data analysis has revealed that the Russian government is using bots to spread skepticism about the safety of vaccines on Twitter in an apparent attempt to create discord in the United States.[5] But many times, negative consequences may well happen inadvertently. *Machine learning* is a type of artificial intelligence that uses computer algorithms to predict, for instance, what products you might like on Amazon or what music you might enjoy on Spotify. According to a recent report in *JAMA Dermatology*, a machine-learning algorithm that distinguishes between images of benign and malignant moles has the potential to spot skin cancers missed by dermatologists.[6] Early skin cancer diagnosis could particularly aid Black patients, who are less likely than White patients to develop melanoma but are more likely to die from it. However, the machine learning algorithms have been trained largely on examples drawn from White patients and are only now being designed in a way that would help control for potential bias.

In this article, I assess changes in the information and data ecosystem that should enable policymakers, researchers, and clinicians to harness this ubiquitous information architecture to identify health disparities, provide a method for evaluating them, and create effective interventions. I point out developments that allow this new technology to move forward at a very fast pace. In addition, I strike a cautious note about the potential negative consequences of the fourth industrial revolution—consequences that may turn advances into a double-edged sword.

Advances in Data & Computing

Recent improvements in society's ability to store and retrieve information, communicate rapidly via digital networks, and analyze data using increasingly powerful methods have fundamentally enlarged the country's capacity to assess and intervene in health disparities. If policymakers, researchers, and clinicians take full advantage of this powerful combination of factors, they will be able to describe people's health in multiple dimensions simultaneously and access information as needed. Combined with navigation systems at the personal, neighborhood, or community level, new analytic data capacities could identify, deal with, and remeasure health problems in a previously unimaginable time frame.

Newly available data sets contain immensely more information about individuals than is currently found in personal health records and other transactions captured by the health care system. Researchers and clinicians are now able to amass novel kinds of biological data, such as an individual's genetic code. With the price of whole-genome sequencing dropping dramatically,[7] scientists can envision a time when this information, consisting of more than 3 billion base pairs, will be routinely available as part of a person's health record. The collection of such biomolecular data could lead to analyses that provide significant insight into the impact of innate biology on a person's health and responses to the physical and social environments.

But purely genomic information is only a small part of the data that can increasingly be used to construct a biomolecular profile. A profile can also include information drawn from transcriptomics (the study of RNA molecules), metabolomics (the study of molecules involved in metabolism), and analyses of the detailed workings of the immune system,[8,9] in addition to integrative physiological information, such as heart rate and blood pressure, that can be measured with digital sensors. Although definitive evidence indicates that social determinants outweigh genetic influences on health risk at a population level, strong evidence also shows that biology has an impact on individual disparities in disease susceptibility and outcome. Further, as described below, when complex data become less expensive to collect, taking a sample or image, recording the information, and digitally storing it for later use becomes much more feasible. Thus, key outputs of a successful data-intensive approach to health disparities will include the delineation of biological mechanisms by which disparities lead to poor health outcomes as well as the development of interventions able to counteract those mechanisms—as was seen in AIR Louisville's efforts to improve asthma control. Such work will also enable the planning of interventions that simultaneously deal with biological and social determinants of health—for example, an asthma intervention that involves both using medications and improving the home environment.

A fast-growing area of health measurement is called *digital phenotyping*,[10] which characterizes people based on the way they interact with cell phones, computers, and other personal devices. This information is deeply informative of the 99% of their lives spent outside of clinics and hospitals. Readily available and increasingly inexpensive sensors in cell phones and watches collect detailed information about individuals continuously over long intervals. Wearable sensors can measure activity levels, tremors, gait, and flexibility. Analyses of keyboard use and gait provide a deep measure of cognitive function, mood, and physical function. Use of cell phone apps and associated social media can provide detailed insights into social activity. Given the dominance of wealth, education, race, and location as mediators of health outcomes, the ability to directly measure behavior and social interactions will provide insights that could not be gained by asking patients questions during visits to a clinic or study site. For example, if your goal is to reduce cardiovascular disease in a population, it may be more important to insert green space and healthy food into neighborhoods than to increase the number of medical clinic visits.

The geospatial dimension is a particularly important factor in health disparities. It generally holds true that the most important predictors of health are zip code and income.[11,12] Current technology allows health outcomes and determinants to be measured at a more granular level: household, street, neighborhood, county, and state levels. This type of measurement feeds into a potential understanding of social networks but also provides a substantial opportunity to make changes in the delivery system for both traditional medicine and social services and then feed information about those changes back to residents of affected neighborhoods and to medical clinicians and social service providers. As the speed of information acquisition, access, and analysis continues to increase, it will be possible to craft interventions at geographical (for example, neighborhood) or social (for example, workplace, school, and church) levels and measure outcomes to fine-tune the interventions (see Figure 1).

The dimension of time is also especially important in gathering individual data. In the past, clinicians and clinical researchers who

---

Key Priorities as Identified by Stakeholders in the Durham Health Innovations Project

- Increase health care coordination and eliminate barriers to services and resources.
- Integrate social, medical, and mental health services.
- Expand health-related services provided in group settings.
- Leverage information technology.
- Use social hubs such as places of worship, community centers, salons, and barbershops as sites for the distribution of clinical and social services and information.
- Increase local access to nurse practitioners, physician assistants, and certified nurse midwives.
- Use traditional marketing methods to influence health behavior.

Note. From "History," by Durham Health Innovations, n.d. (https://sites.duke.edu/durham-healthinnovations/history). Copyright 2015 by Duke Division of Community Health. Reprinted with permission.

Figure 1. Leveraging diverse sources of data to improve population health

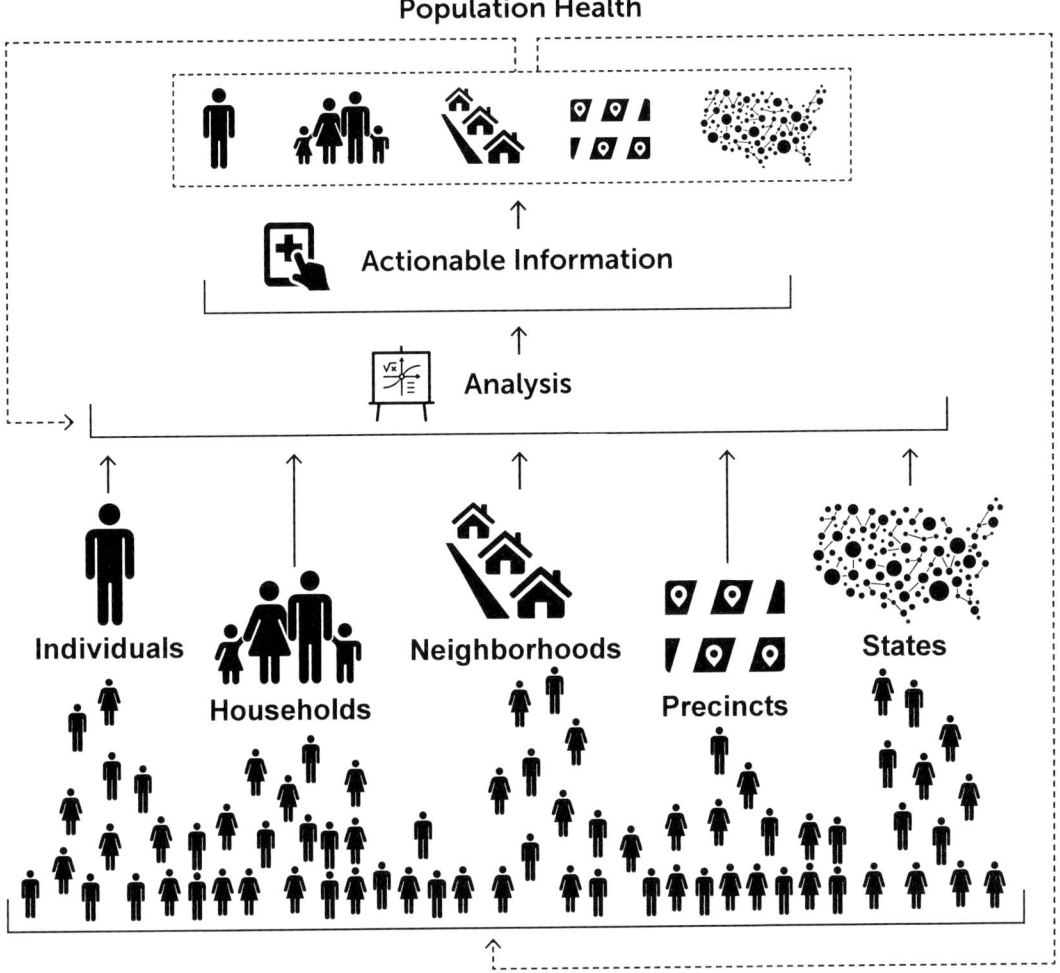

Note. Information from across the spectrum of individual biology, clinical records, behavior, and social interactions can be combined with information about the fixed environment and the ambient environment (bottom). This information is summarized across individuals to produce population-based health measures that can be shared at the levels of the individual, the household, the neighborhood, the voting precinct, and the state. These lead to analysis and actionable information (middle sections). With appropriate analyses, evidence-based policies and interventions that are implemented (top) and assessed with repeated measures (dotted line on the left) can be devised to document the degree of effectiveness of the interventions. The information on more and less effective interventions can then be communicated to individuals and groups such as schools, churches, and neighborhood groups (dotted line on right). The partnership of these stakeholders is essential to the success of the effort.

wanted to evaluate changes over time were limited mostly to measurements made during periodic clinic visits. Digital technologies and the massive increase in the ability to manage data make it possible to use both passive and active data collection to accurately portray the impact of time. Passive measurements, such as the capture of heart rate and physical activity on smart watches and wearable fitness monitors, can be obtained almost continuously. Cell phones can also be used to collect frequent passive impressions from the research participant or patient. As discussed above, this radical reduction in data latency is also pertinent for interventions at the group level, as evidenced by the use of social media to deal with environmental catastrophes.

The study of sleep offers an example of the potential importance of collecting data that cover temporal, spatial, and behavioral dimensions. In the past, this kind of research has relied on either patient recall or intensive study in sleep units, which are artificial environments with little resemblance to the home environment. Now, with passive sensors on wearable technology, the quantity and quality of sleep and attributes of the home environment can be measured without disrupting normal patterns and without great expense to the patient. It is likely that many of the medical, social, and environmental factors that affect sleep are also associated with differences in longevity. Enabled by a system of integrated information such as the one described above, a clinician could intervene at the individual level by prescribing weight loss procedures (to reduce sleep apnea) or sleep medication. Medical institutions, health planners, and legislators could make changes at the group level through social networks or at the geographic and environmental levels by, for instance, reducing noxious sounds by changing traffic patterns.

Harnessing Big Data

The consolidation of clinical care systems, in which big health systems absorb smaller ones, provides opportunities to measure and change health disparities. As of several years ago, the Agency for Healthcare Research and Quality estimated that approximately 650 health systems account for over 90% of hospital discharges and are increasingly integrating hospital and outpatient care, including assisted living, nursing homes, and hospice.[13] These systems are developing sophisticated data "lakes" and warehouses to aggregate information that is curated so that it can show how health care can be delivered in a financially sustainable manner. (The word *curated* deliberately evokes the way historical archives work. Curated data include critical accompanying information about a data point's context—where it was gathered and how it was gathered, stored, transmitted, and transformed, and by whom.)

Because these health systems need standardized information to conduct business, data in several dimensions need to become integrated in a variety of ways. First, the various entities within each system must use common standards and definitions for the system to function efficiently and for patients to benefit from the sharing of information across practices. Second, health care delivery system data should be integrated with information from other dimensions that are pertinent to health—for example, social and environmental factors such as the presence of green spaces, the availability of physicians' offices, and traffic patterns.[2] Third, multiple projects have shown that these data can be merged to produce data sets that can be easily shared across systems, with the goal of improving outcomes.

The National Patient-Centered Clinical Research Network (PCORnet; http://pcornet.org) illustrates the magnitude of data integration that is possible. This project, funded by the Patient-Centered Outcomes Research Institute, has developed a systematic approach to curating data across multiple health systems, including both clinical care data derived from electronic health records and insurance claims data, for over 100 million Americans. PCORnet is now evolving into the People-Centered Research Foundation (http://pcrfoundation.org/), a not-for-profit organization dedicated to conducting pragmatic randomized trials (research performed not at an artificial research center but at a real patient point of contact with an eye to informing decisionmakers of the comparative balance of benefits, burdens, and risks of a biomedical or behavioral health intervention) and observational studies (nonrandomized studies that allow for historical comparisons).

One interesting component of the People-Centered Research Foundation is the ADVANCE Collaborative, a network of federally qualified community health centers.[14] This organization includes OCHIN, Health Choice Network, Fenway Health, Kaiser Permanente Center for Health Research, Legacy Health, CareOregon, and Oregon Health and Science University. Intended as a learning laboratory for policymakers to better understand patients who use safety-net services, the system has digital records on more than 3 million patients, including large numbers of homeless, uninsured, underinsured, and undocumented people, as well as members of other underrepresented populations. This type of network, if coordinated with more traditional integrated health care systems, could provide a mechanism not only for evaluating disparities but also for designing and testing interventions, such as drug counseling, at the system level.

650
Health care systems that account for 90% of all hospital discharges

There are approximately 3 billion base pairs in the human genome.

60%
Health Disparities
Variation in countywide life expectancy due to socioeconomic and race/ethnicity factors

Opportunities for Data to Characterize Disparities

Several organizations are already providing analyses of data that depict health disparities in intuitively understandable displays. Perhaps the most far-reaching of these reports is put out by collaborators working on the Global Burden of Disease Study.[15] Another recent series of reports done mainly at Harvard University has clearly demonstrated that variation in longevity and disease burden in the United States is a function of geographic location at the county level.[16] The striking impact of residence in rural counties is highlighted by the visual depiction of both current longevity and trends in longevity over time. One recent report in this series determined, for instance, that 60% of the variation in countywide life expectancy is explained by socioeconomic and race and ethnicity factors and that rural counties fare worst on such measures as mortality rates, suicides, drug overdose deaths, rates of teenage pregnancy, and fetal and maternal mortality.[12] Detailed analyses of these data have demonstrated that, as expected, wealth, education, race, sex, and location are key factors in longevity,[12] mediated in common chronic diseases by factors such as blood pressure, low physical activity, tobacco use, obesity, depression, and diabetes mellitus.

Many organizations routinely produce comparative reports of health status. Within the United States, significant efforts are aimed at curating actionable data at the level of the city, county, or state. Some of the most potent information comes from the evaluation of boroughs in New York[17] and from state-level reporting by the Robert Wood Johnson Foundation.[18] Research in Durham County, North Carolina, demonstrated the power of this information when it was applied at the level of individual households and neighborhoods to, among other goals, reduce exposure to lead poisoning.[2]

New Ways to Use Data to Reduce Disparities

The same information infrastructure used for measurement could also be used for implementing interventions (See *Key Actions Needed to Collect and Use Actionable Data to Reduce Health Disparities*). At the level of a community or health system, interactions between traditional health systems and social services tend to be inefficient. Improved labeling of government, private, and volunteer services and coordination of these services with clinics, schools, and businesses could lead to a much more directly effective intervention system.

"it should be possible to provide useful information in a way that is tailored to the specific health needs of an individual or family"

In addition, the ubiquity of cell phones and steep reductions in the cost of sensors make it possible for clinicians to communicate directly with individuals and groups at any interval that is desired. Additionally, almost all people use search engines to seek information on a routine basis. Search engine results are tailored by machine-learning algorithms to an individual's pattern of communication. As the curation and organization of information continues to improve, it should be possible to provide useful information in a way that is tailored to the specific health needs of an individual or family. For instance, these approaches can be used to fine-tune search results, much as consumer goods are currently surfaced in a manner consistent with the preferences of the consumer. For example, when someone searches on the term *stage 1 breast cancer*, it is technically possible for the high-ranked results to be tailored to the medical literacy of the individual as well as authoritative, relevant, and trustworthy. For the most common health searches, Google is currently providing "knowledge panels" that are vetted by medical experts.

Consider the ongoing epidemic of asthma. Asthma is often exacerbated by environmental triggers, both within and outside the home. Futher, research has demonstrated that disparities in asthma incidence and access to care are functions of wealth, education, physical location, and race.[19] Inexpensive sensor technology and ubiquitous data networks would enable clinicians to monitor environmental quality at the household and neighborhood levels, which would make it possible for them to deploy precise interventions to reduce stimuli that exacerbate asthma. The previously mentioned report from the study in Louisville[3] points out that this sort of intervention, which focuses on cleaning up the home and neighborhood environments, would potentially be much more powerful than medication in preventing asthma exacerbations.

Similarly, obesity and diabetes contribute to an enormous amount of death and disability, and the geographic and social profiles of relevant health disparities are clear.[20] Although special medical clinics, surgical and medical interventions, and wide dissemination of accurate and useful information that reaches the people who need it are all possible solutions, there is ample reason to believe that constant exposure to advertising for food, long distances to grocery stores that sell healthful food, and cultural and environmental influences on physical activity limit the success of medical interventions for people with lower incomes or other socioeconomic disadvantages. A wealthy, highly educated person who can afford a personal trainer or gym membership and is not caring for family members is more likely to be able to engage in a healthy lifestyle. Health systems, advocacy groups, community leaders, and individuals at all levels of government can engage with people more productively within their personal digital environments, helping them to use geospatial information to locate healthful food resources and enabling and encouraging them to integrate physical activity into their routines in a more economically feasible manner that intrudes less into other aspects of life.

Key Actions Needed to Collect & Use Actionable Data to Reduce Health Disparities

Engage people and communities as partners
- Requires face-to-face time and use of social media
- Transparency is critical at all steps
- Issues of privacy and confidentiality require considerable work

Collect diverse sources of data
- Biological, clinical, behavioral, social, and environmental data are needed
- Full data use will require solutions to engagement, partnership, and privacy/confidentiality issues

Curate and organize data
- Curation and organization are currently the most underinvested area of data science, requiring significant investment
- Requires conscious investment at the institutional level by health systems and government entities

Analyze
- Methods involving geospatial orientation and hierarchical analysis from the level of the individual to population will be informative
- These data are big
- Speed of access to data and fluidity of data are critical factors in making data actionable
- Identifiable data will be most actionable but also riskiest from a privacy/confidentiality perspective

Use outputs of analyses to formulate policies
- Requires collaboration across health systems, neighborhoods, and policymakers at local, state, and national levels
- Participants in the effort need education on quantitative and community engagement methods

Implement policies

Measure again and adjust on the basis of outcomes

Importance of Community Engagement & the Development of Shared Approaches

One area that researchers need to study more thoroughly is how to best transmit new information directly to those who are affected by it as well as to those who can implement interventions and policies to improve outcomes. Although research that engages communities[21] continues to advance, and many communities are involved in direct interventions, policymakers still lack clarity on which methods are likely to be most effective at linking personal health data with social and environmental information in ways that yield measurable improvement in outcomes. A promising approach has been developed by the Abdul Latif Jameel Poverty

Action Lab, which is using observational, experimental, and quasi-experimental methods to understand which social policies lead to improved outcomes.[22] One such study showed that charging fees for preventive medicine tools in low-income countries drastically reduces their usage.[23]

Over a decade ago, Durham County, North Carolina, and Duke University initiated an ambitious program that showed how to create successful communication between government, health institutions, and the community. Called Durham Health Innovations (DHI),[24] the program existed in the context of a history that included decades of both outstanding collaboration between the university and the community and well-documented divisions and disparities.[25] For the project, teams of volunteers were organized so that they had equal representation from the community and the university (including its health system and academic medical center). Each team was focused on addressing a particular health issue of significant concern to the community. Teams were then supported with the data assets of the academic health system, the Durham County public health department, and other entities and asked to devise an approach to health care and community intervention that would improve health outcomes relevant to the issue they had chosen. The teams winnowed their issues down to 10 major problems affecting the community: adolescent health; asthma and chronic obstructive pulmonary disease; cancer prevention and early detection; cardiovascular disease; diabetes; HIV, sexually transmitted diseases, and hepatitis; maternal health; obesity; pain management; and healthy aging in place.[24]

Remarkably, after a series of meetings and discussions aided by intensive data analysis, the proposed approaches to these seemingly different problems all converged on a common set of interventions that could improve the health and health care delivery in Durham regardless of disease or therapeutic area (see *Key Priorities as Identified by Stakeholders in the Durham Health Innovations Project*). The project was ahead of its time and in many ways anticipated the wayfinding approach mentioned

"it is critical that data holders discuss their intentions with the data providers"

in the introduction. It pulled in diverse sources of data to provide a holistic understanding of health needs, with geographic information integrated to guide intervention. But because health data do not enjoy the kind of fluidity and latency advantages leveraged by wayfinding apps, DHI was limited in what it could accomplish. Some of the critical roadblocks to implementing fourth industrial revolution–style solutions can be overcome once project directors can access the right data, in the right way, at the right time.

Steps to Limit the Risks of Data Sharing

Sharing data between patients, physicians, and institutions requires a degree of trust. And clearly, for all the good data sharing can do, a markedly enhanced system of measurement, assessment, and intervention could be used for negative as well as positive purposes. For instance, Facebook's brokerage of personal data during the 2016 U.S. presidential election showed that social media data could be put to nefarious uses.[26] Theoretically, health care information, perhaps hacked from a medical center's patient portal, could be leveraged to, say, target underinsured cancer patients with an ineffective but expensive "cure." False news is particularly dangerous. Empirical evidence is accruing that false statements, many of which are intended to stoke differences among people, reach more people faster and persist longer than truthful statements do because their novelty gives them "legs".[27] These issues are not new, but they have emerged as critical considerations in deciding how to use information to improve the outcomes of those who suffer from health disparities.

To increase transparency, engagement, and trust by patients, clinicians, and institutions, it is critical that data holders discuss their intentions with the data providers. In a body of work on the moral obligations of health systems that are continuously evaluating accruing data to improve health care and health outcomes—that is, *learning health systems*—ethicists Nancy E. Kass and Ruth R. Faden explore a crucial fundamental concept that bears on these challenges: the reciprocal obligation of those who use data to those who provide the data.[28] Although these concepts are reasonable, they have not yet been fully implemented. It is interesting that Kass and Faden's scheme considers reducing disparities to be an essential element of learning health systems.

Given the complexity of interactions needed to successfully implement interventions that reduce health disparities, it will be important for multiple societal entities to involve themselves in developing the cultural and legal expectations that will enable big data to be used effectively for desirable purposes. For example, the current HIPAA laws deal with health care data in a manner that many consider to be overly restrictive, whereas the data from "the other 99%" of life, which have a much larger impact on health outcomes, are governed by much less restrictive rules. Perhaps it would be better to have a single data standard that is pertinent to health outcomes. For this expectation-setting effort to succeed, societal entities that are not motivated by profit and are capable of convening diverse interests should help to devise standards. Universities are in a special position to engage with communities and offer the benefits of faculty knowledge and skills in medicine, law, technology, and ethics as they work with community groups and individuals to devise policies that will achieve the desired results.

A Possible Future

The amount of information now available about individuals and their health—constantly generated and recorded by new, interconnected devices—is multiple log orders more voluminous and complex than the data from patient interactions currently available to clinicians, health care administrators, policymakers, and clinical researchers, and the cost of managing the data is rapidly declining. It is technologically possible to observe, describe, and analyze health disparities at the levels of individuals, households, streets, neighborhoods, cities, and counties. Information-based profiles at each of these levels could be further segregated by biological, medical, behavioral, social, or environmental characteristics. The relevant information that could guide and measure interventions to improve health and reduce health disparities could be displayed in any time interval desired. Interventions could be planned at any of these levels and the results measured in ways that would reveal cause and effect and suggest useful interventions. These same methods, however, if applied for selfish or ignoble purposes, could be leveraged to increase health disparities. Nevertheless, here at the leading edge of the fourth industrial revolution, new methods of data curation and analysis can provide the foundation for a dramatically improved approach to health disparities for both individuals and populations.

author affiliation

Califf: Duke University School of Medicine, Stanford University School of Medicine, and Verily Life Sciences. Corresponding author's e-mail: robert.califf@duke.edu.

references

1. Schwab, K. (2016). The fourth industrial revolution: What it means, how to respond. Retrieved from https://www.weforum.org/agenda/2016/01/the-fourth-industrial-revolution-what-it-means-and-how-to-respond/

2. Miranda, M. L., Ferranti, J., Strauss, B., Neelon, B., & Califf, R. M. (2013). Geographic health information systems: A platform to support the "triple aim." *Health Affairs, 32*, 1608–1615. https://doi.org/10.1377/hlthaff.2012.1199

3. Barrett, M., Combs, V., Su, J. G., Henderson, K., Tuffli, M., & the AIR Louisville Collaborative. (2018). AIR Louisville: Addressing asthma with technology, crowdsourcing, cross-sector collaboration, and policy. *Health Affairs, 37*, 525–534. https://doi.org/10.1377/hlthaff.2017.1315

4. World Bank. (2016). *World development report 2016: Digital dividends*. https://doi.org/10.1596/978-1-4648-0671-1

5. BBC News. (2018, August 24). Russia trolls "spreading vaccination misinformation" to spread discord. Retrieved from http://www.bbc.com/news/world-us-canada-45294192

6. Adamson, A. S., & Smith, A. (2018). Machine learning and health care disparities in dermatology. *JAMA Dermatology*. Advance online publication. https://doi.org/10.1001/jamadermatol.2018.2348

7. National Human Genome Research Institute. (2016). The cost of sequencing a human genome. Retrieved from https://www.genome.gov/27565109/the-cost-of-sequencing-a-human-genome/

8. Institute of Medicine. (2014). *Capturing social and behavioral domains in electronic health records: Phase 1*. Retrieved from http://www.nationalacademies.org/hmd/Reports/2014/Capturing-Social-and-Behavioral-Domains-in-Electronic-Health-Records-Phase-1.aspx

9. Institute of Medicine. (2014). *Capturing social and behavioral domains in electronic health records: Phase 2*. Retrieved from http://www.nationalacademies.org/hmd/Reports/2014/EHRdomains2.aspx

10. Insel, T. R. (2017). Digital phenotyping: Technology for a new science of behavior. *JAMA, 318*, 1215–1216.

11. Chetty, R., Stepner, M., Abraham, S., Lin, S., Scuderi, B., Turner, N., . . . Cutler, D. (2016). The association between income and life expectancy in the United States, 2001–2014. *JAMA, 315*, 1750–1766. https://doi.org/10.1001/jama.2016.4226

12. Dwyer-Lindgren, L., Bertozzi-Villa, A., Stubbs, R. W., Morozoff, C., Mackenbach, J. P., van Lenthe, F. J., . . . Murray, C. J. L. (2017). Inequalities in life expectancy among US counties, 1980 to 2014: Temporal trends and key drivers. *JAMA Internal Medicine, 177*, 1003–1011. https://doi.org/10.1001/jamainternmed.2017.0918

13. Agency for Healthcare Research and Quality. (2016). *Compendium of U.S. health systems, 2016*. Retrieved from https://www.ahrq.gov/chsp/compendium/index.html#data

14. Patient-Centered Outcomes Research Institute. (2017). Accelerating Data Value Across a National Community Health Center Network (ADVANCE). Retrieved from http://pcornet.org/clinical-data-research-networks/cdrn10-oregon-community-health-information-network-ochin/

15. GBD 2016 Causes of Death Collaborators. (2017). Global, regional, and national age-sex specific mortality for 264 causes of death, 1980–2016: A systematic analysis for the Global Burden of Disease Study 2016. *Lancet, 390*, 1151–1210.

16. Murray, C. J. L., Kulkarni, S. C., Michaud, C., Tomijima, N., Bulzacchelli, M. T., Iandiorio, T. J., & Ezzati, M. (2006). Eight Americas: Investigating mortality disparities across races, counties, and race-counties in the United States. *PLoS Medicine, 3*, 1513–1524. https://doi.org/10.1371/journal.pmed.0030260

17. New York City Department of Health and Mental Hygiene. (n.d.). New York City community health profiles. Retrieved from https://www1.nyc.gov/site/doh/data/data-publications/profiles.page

18. Robert Wood Johnson Foundation. (n.d.). County health rankings & roadmaps. Retrieved from https://www.rwjf.org/en/how-we-work/grants-explorer/featured-programs/county-health-ranking-roadmap.html

19. Volerman, A., Chin, M. H., & Press, V. G. (2017). Solutions for asthma disparities. *Pediatrics, 139*, 1–9. https://doi.org/10.1542/peds.2016-2546

20. Centers for Disease Control and Prevention. (2014). *National diabetes statistics report: Estimates of diabetes and its burden in the United States, 2014*. Retrieved April 2, 2015, from https://www.cdc.gov/diabetes/pdfs/data/2014-report-estimates-of-diabetes-and-its-burden-in-the-united-states.pdf

21. Michener, L., Cook, J., Ahmed, S. M., Yonas, M. A., Coyne-Beasley, T., & Aguilar-Gaxiola, S. (2012). Aligning the goals of community-engaged research: Why and how academic health centers can successfully engage with communities to improve health. *Academic Medicine, 87*, 285–291.

22. Abdul Latif Jameel Poverty Action Lab. (n.d.). About us. Retrieved from https://www.povertyactionlab.org/about-j-pal

23. Abdul Latif Jameel Poverty Action Lab. (2018). The impact of price on take-up and use of preventive health products. Retrieved from https://www.povertyactionlab.org/policy-insight/impact-price-take-and-use-preventive-health-products

24. Durham Health Innovations. (n.d.). History. Retrieved from https://sites.duke.edu/durhamhealthinnovations/history

25. Baker, J. P. (2017, September 19). *A tale of two cities? The history of Duke Health and Durham's health* [Video file]. Retrieved from https://dukemed-source.mediasite.com/Mediasite/Play/6b89b77ef0fa465daa848b6e139653ce1d

26. Solon, O. (2018, April 4). Facebook says Cambridge Analytica may have gained 37M more users' data. *The Guardian*. Retrieved from https://www.theguardian.com/technology/2018/apr/04/facebook-cambridge-analytica-user-data-latest-more-than-thought

27. Vosoughi, S., Roy, D., & Aral, S. (2018, March 9). The spread of true and false news online. *Science, 359*, 1146–1151.

28. Faden, R. R., Kass, N. E., Goodman, S. N., Pronovost, P., Tunis, S., & Beauchamp, T. L. (2013). An ethics framework for a learning health care system: A departure from traditional research ethics and clinical ethics. *The Hastings Center Report, 43*(Suppl. 1), S16–S27. https://doi.org/10.1002/hast.134

Using pay-for-success financing for supportive housing interventions: Promise & challenges

Paula M. Lantz & Samantha Iovan

abstract

Pay for success (PFS) is an emerging public–private partnership strategy for providing housing to chronically homeless individuals, people with mental or behavioral disorders, and adults recently released from prison. Socially minded private investors from both for-profit and nonprofit organizations provide the up-front funding for the projects. If an independent evaluation demonstrates that the intervention achieved predetermined metrics of success—such as decreasing the number of days children spend in foster care or increasing the number of people with stable housing—the public sector then "pays for success" by repaying the private investors, sometimes with interest. In this article, we describe seven ongoing PFS housing projects in the United States. Most are "housing first" interventions that provide permanent supportive housing to a chronically homeless population without setting any preconditions, such as sobriety. As projects are completed, analyses of the results should provide further insights into the complexities of designing behavioral-based PFS housing programs.

Lantz, P. M., & Iovan, S. (2018). Using pay-for-success financing for supportive housing interventions: Promise & challenges. *Behavioral Science & Policy, 4*(1), 39–49.

Core Findings

What is the issue?
Pay for success (PFS), or social impact bonds, are an innovative way to improve social outcomes in high-risk communities. Private sector financing is used to implement proven interventions and services, which is repaid by the public sector only when contractual targets for desired outcomes have been met.
The early results from seven PFS projects that provide supportive housing for chronically homeless people are promising illustrations of the PFS financing model.

How can you act?
Selected recommendations include:
1) Building interest and capacity across local and state government agencies to coordinate PFS project buy-in, oversight, and measurement
2) Incentivizing private partners to reinvest success payments back into the PFS project

Who should take the lead?
Advocates, policymakers, government officials, private investors and stakeholders in housing and health

Safe and affordable housing is important for the health and well-being of individuals and communities. Unaffordable housing puts significant economic pressure on individuals and families, forcing them to make stressful trade-offs between, for example, paying rent and buying food, paying utilities, or making investments in their children. Unaffordable housing also leads to eviction and homelessness. A strong body of social science and epidemiological research has demonstrated the positive health effects of housing interventions targeting low-income and vulnerable groups, including the chronically homeless, individuals with mental and behavioral health disorders, and adults recently released from prison.[1] Some of these interventions have also been shown to reduce the amount of money the public sector spends on high-need populations (those who typically have multiple complex medical and social needs and a higher likelihood of chronic homelessness), primarily from reductions in expensive medical, emergency, and criminal justice services.[2]

An emerging funding strategy for social welfare interventions is called *pay for success* (PFS), in which governmental and socially minded private entities (for profit or nonprofit) partner to finance and implement such interventions. Metrics for success are laid out by contract in advance. The private investors initially pay for the program. Then, if a third-party evaluation demonstrates that an intervention has met the contractual criteria for success, the public sector "pays for success" by repaying the private investors, sometimes with interest.[3] The first PFS project was implemented in 2010 in the United Kingdom to reduce criminal recidivism through social and behavioral case management services.[4] Since then, more than 100 PFS projects (also known as *social impact bonds*) have been launched or are being planned worldwide.[5]

The PFS financing model is designed to address two well-known challenges in public administration. The first is government waste, real and perceived. The results-oriented PFS model can reduce inefficiencies and waste because public funds are spent only if specific predetermined, contracted outcomes are achieved. PFS can be used to finance interventions and services that provide value to the public sector. PFS can also be used to conduct a proof-of-concept demonstration of a potentially cost-effective or cost-saving intervention, which in turn might convince government leaders to directly fund such a program in the future.[6]

Second, the PFS financing model addresses the difficulty of investing in preventive interventions with long-term impact when acute public needs urgently require funding. By using private sector capital for up-front financing, PFS allows governments to plan for potential future payouts that are based on the terms of a performance-based contract.[7] This kind of funding is politically attractive to taxpayers—especially when the interventions are aimed at socially marginalized or perceived "undeserving" populations, such as the homeless—because public funds are not used unless the projects succeed.

PFS projects are challenging to establish and launch. In addition, most PFS projects worldwide are still in progress. As such, it is not yet possible to draw conclusions about the impact of PFS projects on social welfare. However, a comprehensive review of the 82 PFS projects launched globally through 2017 revealed that all of them addressed at least one social determinant of health, with the majority implementing educational, behavioral, and psychosocial interventions, including 21 aimed at housing.[8] Through 2017, the PFS financing model garnered more than $390,000,000 of private sector capital for the delivery and evaluation of social welfare interventions, primarily in underserved populations.[5]

In this article, we describe several PFS programs in the United States that focus on an intervention known as *permanent supportive housing*. We also examine the strengths and challenges of the PFS approach to supportive housing in an effort to glean insights into improving those and other PFS programs.

Permanent Supportive Housing Interventions Used in PFS Programs

Permanent supportive housing is a broad term used to describe certain housing interventions aimed at high-risk, high-need populations. These interventions provide long-term housing linked to support services, which are delivered on site or in the community and are meant to improve health and housing stability. Such supports typically include mental and behavioral health care, family interventions, social welfare services, and legal aid. For instance, a woman with a drug dependency problem could receive counseling and support on site and assistance in connecting with other medical and social services in the community. Extensive research has shown that permanent supportive housing can be a cost-saving intervention in high-need populations such as the chronically homeless or adults recently released from prison.[9] These interventions are largely based on theory and research from the fields of health behavior change and social psychology.

Housing first is a specific type of permanent supportive housing program that connects individuals to long-term housing without any sort of precondition, such as sobriety or participation in treatment or services.[10] In other words, the approach ensures that individuals have safe and reliable housing before they attempt to address their social or behavioral challenges. Research shows that supportive services are more effective when individuals choose to participate—as is more likely when no preconditions are set for the receipt of housing—rather than being required to do so.[11]

Some housing first interventions use a *critical time intervention* (CTI) approach, in which individuals receive case management services to assist with the major adjustment that occurs during a move into community housing after being homeless or incarcerated. A social worker or other social services professional pulls together and manages a tailored set of services and resources to meet the individual's needs over time. By receiving support and continuity of care throughout the transition to independent housing, vulnerable individuals should be better able to sustain housing in the long term.[12]

Another way housing first interventions incorporate supportive services is through *assertive community treatment* (ACT). This model of intensive case management includes 24-hour, seven-day-a-week access to individualized care and services. ACT provides intensive support services that are normally available only in inpatient treatment settings. ACT has a strong evidence base behind its ability to provide intensive case management, crisis intervention, substance use counseling, mental health treatment, and primary care referrals. Although originally developed to serve individuals with severe mental illness, ACT has been adapted for and evaluated in a variety of populations.[13]

The Analysis

We designed and implemented a PFS surveillance system in 2016, through which we continuously collect and analyze information on PFS projects that have been launched around the world. This information includes details about the design features, interventions (including the evidence base and relevance to population health), investors, governments involved, metrics of success, payout terms and other contractual elements, evaluation features, outcomes, and challenges.

We collect information only on projects that have officially launched (with a signed contract, secured funding, and actual service delivery) and those in which the back-end payer is a government entity. Although a number of other websites describe PFS activity, we go further

> "permanent supportive housing can be a cost-saving intervention in high-need populations"

by using descriptive project data to follow the research, administrative, policy, and population impacts of PFS initiatives.[14] In this article, we use our PFS surveillance data to describe key elements of the housing projects underway in the United States and to identify some of the strengths and challenges of using the PFS financing model for supportive housing interventions in low-income populations.

This second aspect of our article includes an assessment of whether PFS housing projects generally meet established criteria for using PFS programs to improve social welfare, such as having a strong evidence base behind the chosen interventions.[15] Many resources, including the Urban Institute's Project Assessment Tool, provide guidance for developing successful PFS projects.[16] Projects that are most likely to succeed should meet the following criteria:

- The intervention must address a problem of interest to the public sector.

- The intervention should have published evidence of effectiveness in a clearly identified population.

- The intervention should provide economic value to the public sector by being either cost-effective or cost saving.

- Outcomes must be clearly defined and measurable.

- Outcomes must be achievable in a reasonable time period.

- Outcomes must be achievable without significant administrative, political, or stakeholder challenges, such as objections from local leadership, project partners, or the community.[15]

Our description and analysis of PFS housing interventions should be useful for government leaders and socially minded investors who are exploring potential PFS initiatives in and beyond supportive housing.

PFS Supportive Housing Projects in the United States

As of May 1, 2018, 21 housing-related PFS projects have been launched globally, of which seven (33%) are in the United States.[8] At least 11 additional PFS housing projects are in development in the United States, including projects funded through the U.S. Department of Housing and Urban Development's Pay for Success Permanent Supportive Housing Demonstration initiative.[17] Next, we summarize the seven established PFS housing projects in the United States, providing a comparison of the major components of each contract in Table 1.

Partnering for Family Success, Cuyahoga County, Ohio. The Partnering for Family Success project aims to reduce the number of days in foster care for children whose caregivers are homeless.[18] In 2014, the year this program launched, Cuyahoga County budgeted more than $50 million for foster care.[19] By providing homeless parents with stable housing, the county hopes to improve the well-being of homeless families while also saving money. In addition to a housing first intervention, clients receive CTI, trauma-adapted family connections, and child–parent psychotherapy, three psychosocial interventions aimed at improving relationships within families, taking into account the traumatic context of their current or past situations.[20,21]

This project will serve 135 homeless families over a five-year period, with the aim of reducing foster care placement days by 25%. If that is achieved, investors will receive full repayment of their investment. If the target is exceeded, investors will be repaid with interest. Investors have stated that they plan to reinvest any success payments back into the program, which will provide long-term funding and sustainability.

Chronic Homelessness PFS Initiative, Massachusetts. To address the issue of homelessness and the costly use of public services, Massachusetts launched a PFS project in 2015 to deliver the Home & Healthy for Good (HHG) program to chronically homeless individuals.[22] Using a housing first approach to address the high usage of emergency services by chronically

Table 1. Key components of initiatives related to pay-for-success supportive housing in the United States, May 2018

Variable	Project						
	Partnering for Family Success	Chronic Homelessness PFS Initiative	Project Welcome Home	Housing to Health	Homes Not Jail	REACH	Just in Reach
Government	Cuyahoga County, Ohio	Commonwealth of Massachusetts	Santa Clara County, California	Denver, Colorado	Salt Lake County, Utah	Salt Lake County, Utah	Los Angeles County, California
Duration	5 years	5 years	6 years	5 years	6 years	6 years	4 years
Total investment	$4M	$3.5M	$6.9M	$8.6M	$5.3M	$5.4M	$10M
Investors	George Gund Foundation, Cleveland Foundation, Sisters of Charity Foundation of Cleveland, Laura and John Arnold Foundation, Reinvestment Fund, Nonprofit Finance Fund	Santander Bank, United Way of Massachusetts Bay and Merrimack Valley, Corporation for Supportive Housing	Reinvestment Fund, Corporation for Supportive Housing, Sobrato Family Foundation, California Endowment, Health Trust, James Irvine Foundation, Google.org	Northern Trust, Walton Family Foundation, Piton Foundation, Laura and John Arnold Foundation, Living Cities, Nonprofit Finance Fund	Northern Trust, Ally Bank, QBE Insurance, Reinvestment Fund, Sorenson Impact Foundation	Northern Trust, Ally Bank, QBE Insurance, Reinvestment Fund, Sorenson Impact Foundation	United Healthcare, Conrad N. Hilton Foundation
Service delivery organization(s)	FrontLine Service	Massachusetts Housing and Shelter Alliance	Adobe Services	Colorado Coalition for the Homeless, Mental Health Center of Denver, Colorado Access	The Road Home	First Step House	L.A. County Department of Health Services, Brilliant Corners
Other housing organizations	Enterprise Community Partners	N/A	N/A	Enterprise Community Partners, Corporation for Supportive Housing	N/A	N/A	Corporation for Supportive Housing
Intervention	Housing First, Critical Time Intervention, Trauma Adapted Family Connections, child-parent psychotherapy	Home & Healthy for Good, Housing First supportive housing	Housing First, Assertive Community Treatment	Housing First, Assertive Community Treatment	Rapid Re-Housing (Housing First supportive housing), trauma-informed care, motivational interviewing	Risk–Needs–Responsivity Model	Housing First supportive housing
Target population	Homeless caregivers with children in foster care	Chronically homeless	Chronically homeless	Chronically homeless	Chronically homeless with substance use disorders	Formerly incarcerated adults	Chronically homeless
Success metric(s)	Reduction in foster care days	12 months of continuous housing	3 months of continuous stable tenancy	365 total adjusted days in housing, reduction in jail bed days	Improvement in the number of months without being in jail or the shelter, graduation to permanent housing, substance abuse treatment enrollment, mental health treatment enrollment	Reduction in days incarcerated, reduction in statewide arrests, increase in employment, program engagement	6 months and 12 months in stable housing, reduction in arrests

homeless individuals with complex needs, HHG was created in 2006 to provide health, social, and behavioral support after individuals are placed into housing. Since its inception, HHG has assisted 973 formerly homeless individuals with permanent supportive housing in Massachusetts, resulting in an average annual savings of $12,428 per tenant housed, according to a state Medicaid analysis.[23]

The Chronic Homelessness PFS Initiative represents a scaling of the HHG services already delivered by the Massachusetts state government. Over the five-year PFS project period, supportive housing will be provided to approximately 800 chronically homeless individuals. Repayment to private investors depends on participants achieving housing stability for 12 months. If 80% of individuals meet this milestone, investors will receive full repayment of their principal investment from the state. If more than 80% of project participants achieve 12 months of continuous housing, investors will be repaid with interest. First-year outcomes revealed a housing retention rate of 92%, resulting in an interim repayment to investors (see Table 2 for additional reported results).

Project Welcome Home, Santa Clara County, California. Project Welcome Home was launched in 2015 to provide supportive housing to chronically homeless individuals living in Santa Clara County.[24] The project targets adults identified as high-cost users of county services like emergency care, inpatient care, and criminal justice system resources. This project combines housing first and the ACT model of intensive case management to address a wide range of social and behavioral needs. Project Welcome Home will ultimately serve 150–200 chronically homeless individuals over the course of the six-year project. Success payments will initiate when a participant reaches a minimum of three months of continuous stable tenancy. The goal of Project Welcome Home is for 80% of participants to achieve 12 months of continuous tenancy.

Housing to Health, Denver, Colorado. The Denver Housing to Health initiative was launched in 2016 to address the high use of expensive city and county safety-net services by chronically homeless individuals.[25] Housing to Health is using a housing first approach to provide 250 residential units to chronically homeless individuals over the five-year project period. As in Project Welcome Home, service providers are using ACT intensive case management to provide supportive services to enrollees.

The Housing to Health initiative is being evaluated with respect to two outcomes: housing stability and jail days. Housing stability payments will be calculated on the basis of total adjusted days in housing for each individual who reaches a threshold of at least 365 days housed in the community. Jail reduction payments are based on the reduction of jail days in the intervention participants, with a minimum threshold of a greater than 20% reduction in jail days compared with a control group.

Table 2. Interim payout & results data from the Chronic Homelessness PFS Initiative in Massachusetts

Project Feature	Characteristic or result
Project launch date	June 2015
Total investment	$2,500,000
Investors (amount invested)	Santander Bank ($1,000,000) United Way of Massachusetts Bay and Merrimack Valley ($1,000,000) Corporation for Supportive Housing ($500,000)
First success payments to investors announced	February 2018
Participants housed (through 2/2018)	656
Participants meeting success metric (through 2/2108)	92% of participants remained permanently housed 1 year after placement
Success payments to investors (through 2/2018)	Santander Bank ($102,200) United Way of Massachusetts Bay and Merrimack Valley ($102,200) Corporation for Supportive Housing ($51,000)

Homes Not Jail, Salt Lake County, Utah. The Homes Not Jail project was launched in 2017 in Salt Lake County to serve persistently homeless adults with substance use disorders. Homes Not Jail uses a housing first intervention called *rapid rehousing* that provides individuals with fast-paced move-in support, rental assistance, peer support, and financial and case management services.[26] Homes Not Jail explicitly uses a harm-reduction approach, allowing participants who are currently struggling with substance abuse to obtain housing without any social or behavioral preconditions. Motivational interviewing and trauma-informed care are also used to help participants make positive behavioral and psychosocial changes. As with the other PFS housing interventions, service delivery partners provide comprehensive wraparound services to assist with lingering social issues, such as food insecurity and unemployment.

Over the six-year project period, Homes Not Jail will serve 315 persistently homeless individuals in Salt Lake County. Four outcomes will serve as measures of success: months without staying in a shelter or jail, mental health service participation, substance abuse service enrollment, and graduation to permanent supportive housing. Any significant improvement in the first three measures relative to a control group will result in a payment. Payment for graduating to permanent supportive housing is made for each participant who is living in permanent housing when discharged from the program. The project goals are a 30% improvement for participants in the number of months without a stay in jail or a shelter and 80% of participants graduating to permanent housing.

REACH, Salt Lake County, Utah. REACH (Recovery, Engagement, Assessment, Career, and Housing), launched in 2017, is a broad-based intervention tailored specifically to the needs of formerly incarcerated adult men who are currently under the supervision of Utah Adult Probation & Parole.[26,27] The REACH program uses the risk–need–responsivity model, which takes into account the risk a person will reoffend and his other specific social, behavioral, psychosocial, and structural needs.[28] Participants receive individualized services such as short-term housing, case management, substance abuse treatment, mental health services, and employment support.

REACH will eventually serve approximately 225 formerly incarcerated individuals over the six-year project. Success payments are determined on the basis of four outcomes among participants: reduction in the number of days incarcerated, reduction in the number of statewide arrests, improvement in the number of quarters of employment, and successful program engagement. Any significant improvement in the first three outcomes compared with a control group will result in success payments to investors.

Just in Reach, Los Angeles County, California. Los Angeles County launched the Just in Reach PFS initiative in 2017 to reduce recidivism and end the cycle of homelessness among individuals with repeat county jail stays.[29] This housing first program links chronically homeless individuals to permanent supportive housing. Once participants enter stable housing, they are provided with social, behavioral, and health services, including mental health therapy, substance abuse treatment, employment services, connections to public benefits, and mentors. A 2008 demonstration project showed a significant decrease in the recidivism rate for program participants compared with the general jail population.[30]

The Just in Reach PFS initiative aims to serve 300 homeless individuals who are currently in the county jail; have had prior jail stays; and have complex social or behavioral problems such as mental illness, substance use disorder, or posttraumatic stress disorder. The four-year project will make payments on the basis of housing retention and jail avoidance rates. Housing retention payments will be made for each participant who reaches six months and then 12 months in stable housing. The jail avoidance rate is based on the number of rearrests during the two years following entry into supportive housing, with success payments based on participants with two or fewer returns to jail in a two-year follow-up period.

$390m
PFS capital raised through the private sector in 2017

25.6
Percentage of PFS projects worldwide aimed at housing, through 2017

33%
of current PFS housing projects worldwide are in the U.S.

"Both nonprofit and for-profit investors have provided capital"

Summary. Although the seven PFS housing projects have differences, they all include the delivery of evidence-based interventions to marginalized or vulnerable groups with complex needs. With the exception of REACH in Salt Lake County, all the projects use a housing first approach combined with some variant of permanent or long-term supportive housing. They deliver a range of supportive services to address the complex psychosocial, behavioral, and medical needs of the target population. Both nonprofit and for-profit investors have provided capital, and key agencies and organizations in the field of housing, including the Corporation for Supportive Housing, the Reinvestment Fund, and Enterprise Community Partners, have been involved in many of the projects. Success payments to the private investors are contingent on some measure of sustained housing in all but two projects (Partnering for Family Success in Cuyahoga County and REACH in Salt Lake County).

The Big Picture

The PFS financing model is being used by governments and private entities to support the dissemination of evidence-based interventions. The projects described here provide models for how this public–private financing approach has been implemented in the important area of housing. Private nonprofit and for-profit investors have demonstrated interest in investing in evidence-based supportive housing interventions, bringing new sources of private revenue to address housing in high-risk, complex-need populations. Although PFS is in the early stages of development, evidence presented here and elsewhere suggests it holds promise as a way to finance housing, a critical component of health and social equity.[14]

Strengths. A clear strength of the seven PFS housing projects we have described is that they meet the minimum criteria for interventions appropriate for PFS, as described earlier.[15] Not all launched PFS projects have met these criteria.

All the PFS housing projects to date in the United States address a problem of interest to the public sector by implementing cost-effective and perhaps even cost-saving interventions that have a strong research evidence base in the target populations. What is more, the project outcomes are clear, measurable, and achievable in a reasonable time period (four to six years) and do not appear to have serious stakeholder challenges. However, the administrative costs of these projects are currently not well understood. In addition, the final outcomes from these projects (including investor payouts) are not yet known. Only two projects thus far have resulted in interim payouts to investors. Nevertheless, these interventions, if implemented with fidelity to the intervention research literature, should be able to achieve their objectives.

It is important to note that in all seven PFS housing projects in the United States to date, the payouts are contractually based on the achievement of behavioral outcomes, such as stable housing, treatment enrollment, and lack of recidivism—not on evidence of public savings. This is a major strength of this approach for making social progress.

Challenges. Even though the research literature suggests that supportive housing interventions save money that is often spent on high-risk populations, there are significant administrative and legal challenges to explicitly capturing public savings. These include the "wrong pockets" problem, in which the savings from a PFS initiative accrue across multiple government agencies and their budgets, which makes it difficult to identify and capture savings for the purpose of repaying private investors. Furthermore, legal barriers can prohibit some government programs (such as the federal arm of Medicaid) from making success payments to private investors.[14]

Additional challenges can complicate growing or scaling up the PFS financing model for supportive housing. One is the need for the government to increase its interest and capacity for engaging in PFS activity, which is a unique type of results-driven contracting. Local and state governments need capacity in a number of key areas—including leadership buy-in, procurement policies, contract management, and the data systems for measuring outcomes and cost-effectiveness.[6,31]

Another challenge is that even though success payments do not depend on the government saving money, to be economically attractive for PFS financing, housing interventions must target individuals at the highest risk of needing expensive public services, such as chronically homeless populations with mental health, substance abuse, and other disabling problems. Although such individuals are in obvious need of supportive housing, this focus on those at highest risk is open to the criticism that such programs neglect individuals and families who are also in need of stable, affordable, and supportive housing but who are not high users of costly public services. As a public–private partnership financing model, however, PFS is best suited for interventions that provide significant economic efficiencies or savings to the public sector and thus are bound to target the outlying, highest need populations.

Third, given the challenges that local and state governments face in funding expensive interventions like permanent supportive housing, the long-term sustainability of these interventions depends on maintaining the enthusiasm of private and public sector participants. To sustain an intervention, either the investors must be willing to reinvest success payments back into the project or the public sector must itself take over the financing and oversight of the intervention. Although such interest is increasing among health care systems, Medicaid managed care organizations, public health agencies, and researchers, using Medicaid mechanisms to finance housing and other social and nonmedical interventions related to health can be problematic because of significant administrative obstacles.[32]

Looking Ahead

In summary, despite the challenges, PFS remains an important way to finance housing interventions in populations that are high users of government programs and services. PFS

> "A clear strength of the seven PFS housing projects . . . is that they meet the minimum criteria for interventions appropriate for PFS"

housing-related projects implemented to date provide excellent examples of how this financing model can enable the spread of evidence-based permanent supportive housing that improves housing stability and other outcomes. The long-term social, behavioral, and health impacts of the PFS housing projects that are underway are not yet known, but it does appear that PFS has opened the door for evidence-based program delivery to populations who may not otherwise be served via traditional funding mechanisms. Although the early results are promising, the final evaluations of these pioneering projects will more fully reveal the potential of PFS financing for behavioral-based supportive housing and other social welfare interventions in high-need populations.

author affiliations

Lantz & Iovan: University of Michigan, Ford School of Public Policy. Corresponding author's e-mail: plantz@umich.edu.

author note

This work was supported by an award from the Robert Wood Johnson Foundation (award 73217) for the University of Michigan Policies for Action Research Hub.

references

1. Gibson, M., Petticrew, M., Bambra, C., Sowden, A. J., Wright, K. E., & Whitehead, M. (2011). Housing and health inequalities: A synthesis of systematic reviews of interventions aimed at different pathways linking housing and health. *Health & Place, 17,* 175–184.

2. Ly, A., & Latimer, E. (2015). Housing First impact on costs and associated cost offsets: A review of the literature. *The Canadian Journal of Psychiatry, 60,* 475–487.

3. Galloway, I. (2014). Using pay-for-success to increase investment in the nonmedical determinants of health. *Health Affairs, 33,* 1897–1904.

4. Ministry of Justice. (2017). *Peterborough social impact bond: Background.* Retrieved from https://assets.publishing.service.gov.uk/government/uploads/system/uploads/attachment_data/file/633271/peterborough-social-impact-bond-background-information.pdf

5. Social Finance. (n.d.). Impact bond global database. Retrieved from https://sibdatabase.socialfinance.org.uk/

6. Whistler, C. (2017). The next phase of pay for success: Driving public sector outcomes. Retrieved from https://www.thirdsectorcap.org/blog/the-next-phase-of-pay-for-success-driving-public-sector-outcomes/

7. Carrillo, O. (2017). *Pay for success: Opportunities and challenges in housing and economic development.* Retrieved from http://www.jchs.harvard.edu/sites/default/files/carrillo_pay_for_success_gramlich_2017.pdf

8. Iovan, S., Lantz, P. M., & Shapiro, S. (2018). "Pay for success" projects: Financing interventions that address social determinants of health in 20 countries. *American Journal of Public Health, 108,* 1473–1477.

9. Office of the Assistant Secretary for Planning and Evaluation. (2014). 3.1. Permanent supportive housing and services for people experiencing chronic homelessness. In *A primer on using Medicaid for people experiencing chronic homelessness and tenants in permanent supportive housing.* Retrieved from https://aspe.hhs.gov/report/primer-using-medicaid-people-experiencing-chronic-homelessness-and-tenants-permanent-supportive-housing

10. HUD Exchange. (2014). *Housing First in permanent supportive housing.* Retrieved from https://www.hudexchange.info/resources/documents/Housing-First-Permanent-Supportive-Housing-Brief.pdf

11. National Alliance to End Homelessness. (2016). Housing First. Retrieved from https://endhomelessness.org/resource/housing-first/

12. Social Programs That Work. (2017). Evidence summary for the critical time intervention. Retrieved from https://evidencebasedprograms.org/document/critical-time-intervention-evidence-summary/

13. Phillips, S. D., Burns, B. J., Edgar, E. R., Mueser, K. T., Linkins, K. W., Rosenheck, R. A., . . . McDonel Herr, E. C. (2001). Moving assertive community treatment into standard practice. *Psychiatric Services, 52,* 771–779.

14. Lantz, P. M., Rosenbaum, S., Ku, L., & Iovan, S. (2016). Pay for success and population health: Early results from eleven projects reveal challenges and promise. *Health Affairs, 35,* 2053–2061.

15. Lantz, P. M., & Iovan, S. (2017, December 12). When does pay-for-success make sense? *Stanford Social Innovation Review.* Retrieved from https://ssir.org/articles/entry/when_does_pay_for_success_make_sense

16. Milner, J., Eldridge, M., Walsh, K., & Roman, J. K. (2016). *Pay for success project assessment tool.* Retrieved from https://www.urban.org/sites/default/files/publication/85391/pay-for-success-project-assessment-tool_1.pdf

17. U.S. Department of Housing and Urban Development. (2015). *Pay for Success Permanent Supportive Housing Demonstration* [Fact sheet]. Retrieved from https://www.hudexchange.info/resources/documents/PFS-Demonstration-Fact-Sheet.pdf

18. Enterprise Community Partners & Third Sector Capital Partners. (2016). *Developing the Cuyahoga Partnering for Family Success Program.* Retrieved from https://www.thirdsectorcap.org/wp-content/uploads/2016/02/Final-Cuyahoga-Partnering-for-Family-Success-Program-Lessons-Learned-Report.pdf

19. FitzGerald, E. (2013). *Cuyahoga County, Ohio 2014–2015 executive's recommended biennial budget.* Retrieved from http://council.cuyahogacounty.us/pdf_council/en-US/2014-2015Budget/2014-2015%20Recommended%20Budget_2.pdf

20. National Child Traumatic Stress Network. (2012). *TA-FC: Trauma adapted family connections* [Fact sheet]. Retrieved from https://www.nctsn.org/sites/default/files/interventions/tafc_fact_sheet.pdf

21. Bassuk, E. L., DeCandia, C. J., Tsertsvadze, A., & Richard, M. K. (2014). The effectiveness of housing interventions and housing and service interventions on ending family homelessness: A systematic review. *American Journal of Orthopsychiatry, 84,* 457–474.

22. Pulster, R. (2015). Massachusetts launches pay for success initiative to address chronic homelessness. Retrieved from https://www.usich.gov/news/massachusetts-launches-pay-for-success-initiative-to-address-chronic-homele

23. Massachusetts Housing and Shelter Alliance. (2018). *Permanent supportive housing: A solution-driven model. March 2018 Home & Healthy for Good progress report.* Retrieved from https://www.mhsa.net/sites/default/files/March%202018%20HHG%20Report.pdf

24. County of Santa Clara. (2017). *County of Santa Clara launches California's first "pay for success" project* [Press release]. Retrieved from https://www.sccgov.org/sites/opa/nr/Pages/ProjectWelcomeHome.aspx

25. Corporation for Supportive Housing. (2016). *Fact sheet: Denver social impact bond program to address homelessness.* Retrieved from https://www.csh.org/wp-content/uploads/2011/12/Denver-SIB-FactSheet.pdf

26. Salt Lake County Council. (2017). Pay for success reports: December 2017 update. Retrieved from https://slco.org/council/pay-for-success-reports/

27. Salt Lake County. (2016). *Fact sheet: Salt Lake County pay for success initiatives.* Retrieved from https://slco.org/uploadedFiles/depot/fMayor/mayor16/PFS_launch_Factsheet.pdf

28. Bonta, J., & Andrews, D. A. (2007). Risk-need-responsivity model for offender assessment and rehabilitation. *Rehabilitation, 6,* 1–22.

29. Corporation for Supportive Housing. (2017). "Just in Reach" supportive housing. Retrieved from https://www.csh.org/2017/10/just-in-reach-supportive-housing/

30. Los Angeles County Sheriff's Department, Community Transition Unit. (YEAR). Just in Reach (JIR) Services for Homeless Inmates. Retrieved from http://www.naco.org/sites/default/files/documents/Session%204%20-%20Los%20Angeles%20County%20Sheriff's%20Department.pdf

31. Harvard Kennedy School Government Performance Lab. (2016). *Results-driven contracting: An overview.* Retrieved from http://govlab.hks.harvard.edu/files/siblab/files/results-driven_contracting_an_overview_0.pdf

32. McGinnis, T., Bonney, J., & Chang, D. I. (2018). *Executive summary: Innovative Medicaid payment strategies for upstream prevention and population health.* Retrieved from http://www.chcs.org/media/Innovative-Medicaid-Payment-Strategies-for-Upstream-Prevention-and-Population-Health.pdf

Improving the match between patients' needs & end-of-life care by increasing patient choice in Medicare

Donald H. Taylor, Jr.

abstract

One way to achieve *health equity*—ensuring everyone has fair and just opportunities to be as healthy as possible—in the United States would be to reallocate Medicare spending from low-value medical care (expensive treatments that do little good) toward high-value medical and social care (respectively, medical interventions that have been shown to work well but are not covered by Medicare and nonmedical interventions, such as help with activities of daily living, that patients find more helpful than low-value care). In the current policy milieu, the most practical, direct step in that direction may be for Medicare—an already established, universal health care program for the elderly—to provide patients with more choices and autonomy.

Taylor, D. H., Jr. (2018). Improving the match between patients' needs & end-of-life care by increasing patient choice. *Behavioral Science & Policy, 4*(1), 51–61.

Core Findings

What is the issue?
U.S. health outcomes lag behind those of other developed countries despite high levels of health care investment. Public spending investments through Medicare tend to cover low-value end-of-life medical care and not broader high-value care alternatives that include social service options. An evidence-based shift toward these options can serve both efficiency and equity in health outcomes.

How can you act?
Selected recommendations include:
1) Identifying specific medical conditions that frequently result in low-value care provision
2) Testing the efficacy of covering lump sums as an end-of-life health care alternative, to encourage use of social services like home nursing and transportation for doctor visits

Who should take the lead?
Researchers, policymakers, and stakeholders in health care

Well-documented inequalities in health insurance coverage, access to care, and population health clearly show that the United States has far to go to reach anything approaching *health equity*—a goal the Robert Wood Johnson Foundation has defined as everyone having "a fair and just opportunity to be as healthy as possible."[1] What are the best approaches for moving toward health equity?

In this article, I propose that the most direct and far-reaching action that might be achievable in the current political climate would be for Medicare, which offers medical coverage to everyone 65 years of age and older, to shift away from primarily covering and promoting medical care services near the end of life that often turn out to be low value, and instead move toward enabling patients to receive high-value medical care and social services paid for by Medicare. By *low-value medical care services*, I mean expensive medical interventions that do little good, such as delivering last-ditch chemotherapy to a cancer patient who has little chance of responding and who is more likely to be harmed by side effects than helped. By *high-value medical care and social services*, I mean medical care that has been shown to work well but that is not directly financed by Medicare, such as comfort-focused palliative care given before a patient elects to receive hospice care and forgo curative therapy, and nonmedical services, such as meal preparation or help with transportation to doctors' offices, that tend to be less expensive than medical care and are more predictably beneficial to elderly persons across many health circumstances.

The need for changes in health-related spending is undeniable. The United States invests a great deal in health care: the nation's expenditure on health care, which represents around half of the country's total spending, is approximately equivalent to the combined governmental and private spending in most high-income nations. Yet the United States has only middling population-level health outcomes.[2] This pattern has often been viewed as evidence that inequality in access to and use of care leads to poor outcomes, but that is not the whole explanation. Research conducted by Elizabeth H. Bradley and Lauren Taylor of Yale University[3] shows that lack of investment in social services that affect health—such as education, income support, housing, nutrition, and child care—explains a substantial portion of the nation's poor health in spite of its high health care spending. What Taylor and Bradley have called "the national investment in health"—the combined money devoted to health care and social services—is merely average compared with that of the other nations in the Organisation for Economic Co-operation and Development. A middling national investment in health yields middling health outcomes.

Bradley and Taylor[3] concluded that policymakers concerned with health equity should broaden their focus beyond simply expanding access to health insurance and should work to expand social interventions. The important effects of social factors on health are well documented and may explain over half the variation in observed health outcomes between nations and between groups within nations.[4-6]

In spite of ample evidence that health outcomes are influenced by many factors, for the last decade, the health policy focus in Washington, DC, has primarily centered on passing (or opposing) and implementing (or sabotaging) the Affordable Care Act (ACA), which prioritized expanding insurance coverage to nonelderly individuals who lacked access to employer-sponsored health insurance, a relatively small slice of the overall population. The controversy generated by this fairly narrow reform, which was nevertheless the most comprehensive since the creation of Medicare and Medicaid in 1965, demonstrates how difficult large-scale efforts to disrupt the status quo can be.

One could imagine an alternative policy initiative that invests the same magnitude of resources into social services for children, for example. The ACA was financed by a mix of cuts in reimbursement to the Medicare program and increased taxes. If the same money were instead invested in social services, funding better education and housing for low-income children, the allocation would move the nation's investment in health in a direction that the social science and public health literatures suggest is conducive to better societal-level health outcomes,[6-8] such as more children going on to earn good incomes and living in healthier conditions.

A shift from spending on the elderly toward spending on children might be expected to have the biggest bang for the buck in moving the U.S. population toward health equity. Such a shift would, of course, be politically impossible in the United States today, where the elderly advocate powerfully for the health care complex that provides them with care and where the government is currently inclined to cut social spending.

Yet shifting expenditures within the Medicare program from the kind of health care that is often delivered near the end of a person's life to other medical care and social services would probably be more politically feasible and would better meet the needs of many, as I argue in this article. I also describe ways to determine which services people prefer and to discover whether shifting Medicare coverage in this direction would, in fact, improve outcomes while increasing the autonomy and participation of the elderly in determining the best ways to address their illnesses and disabilities.

Why Shifting Away From Low-Value Medical Care Near the End of Life Makes Policy Sense

One reason to focus on care delivered near the end of life is that the United States overspends on low-value care at that time, as abundant evidence indicates. Since 1970, one in four Medicare dollars has been spent during the last year of a Medicare beneficiary's life.[9] Yet the expensive care that is provided in a person's last days, weeks, or months often does not extend life or improve other health outcomes and may even harm patients.[10,11] Many families experience regret over care choices made for loved ones just before death, and studies have documented posttraumatic stress disorder in survivors who witness a loved one die in an intensive care unit.[12-14]

The kinds of changes I am recommending could apply, for instance, to an elderly person suffering from advanced heart failure, which has no clear medical therapy to cure the disease, or to a patient with lung cancer who has already tried the existing chemotherapy and radiation treatments. There is almost always something else to try medically, but I am proposing to allow patients to decide when they have had enough medical care that is not working and to instead use their Medicare coverage to pay for other types of care or social services that would be more likely to improve their quality of life.

A change in Medicare policy that reallocated money within the program to make changes driven by patient choices might be more palatable to policymakers than other proposals for improving health outcomes in the United States because it would not require added funding or creating a new program. The approach would benefit many elderly patients—a growing segment of the population—and potentially reduce health inequity between disadvantaged and advantaged senior citizens. For instance, shifting resources from low-value medical care to social services in a program that already covers everyone after they reach the age of 65 years could help to compensate for long-standing sources of inequity, including race, income, education, and rural residence, in that age group. No similar universal insurance structure exists for younger persons. In addition, given that much spending by Medicare near the end of life is of questionable value, the approach has the potential to reallocate some program spending without the change being detrimental to one group while benefiting another.

The proposal has another benefit as well: if evidence-based reallocation of low-value medical spending to high-value social spending could be achieved in Medicare by enabling patients to play a larger role in determining their own care, that accomplishment could catalyze considerations of similar reallocations in other programs that could improve health equity.

There is a problem with directing a policy toward the end of life: the "end of life" concept is

> "most people in a given clinical situation will not benefit from last-ditch medical treatment"

inherently retrospective. In other words, you do not know when the last year of life started until it ends. Predicting death involves a great deal of uncertainty, even for very sick elderly patients, and so it it is impossible to design policies that specifically address the last year or months of patients' lives prospectively, which is the only way to change observed spending patterns. Indeed, physicians often do not know how long a person will survive or whether a given intervention is futile. As Lisa Rosenbaum of Brigham and Women's Hospital noted in a recent essay[15] that pushed back against what she termed the "less-is-more crusade" in treatment, "sometimes less is more, sometimes more is more, and often we just don't know."

A recent analysis of Medicare claims data supports quantitatively Rosenbaum's caution about the difficulty of predicting who will die, even among seriously ill elderly persons.[16]

The provider's dilemma—how to decide what to do in the face of uncertainty about, on the one hand, any given individual's prognosis and, on the other hand, reasonable evidence that most people in a given clinical situation will not benefit from last-ditch medical treatment—can be addressed in part by providing better information and additional care options to patients who are afforded the autonomy to make their own decisions with the best information available. This approach is also the most plausible way to address a common two-sided learning problem that contributes to the perpetuation of Medicare-funded low-value-care delivery. In the balance of this article, I outline a process for addressing such problems, one that keeps research evidence and patient preferences at the fore of attempts to reform the system.

Why End-of-Life Care Has Been Hard to Change

One part of the two-sided learning problem standing in the way of better end-of-life care is summarized by the truism "your mother only dies once." That is, after a loved one dies, family members and other caregivers who learned how to navigate health care decisions for the patient often do nothing with their hard-won wisdom. There are no clear feedback mechanisms through which they can share knowledge with those who are beginning the same journey, and so a wealth of practical knowledge is lost.

The second part of the problem is the converse of the first: the health care system copes repeatedly with people near the end of their life (after all, everyone dies!), and providers can see after the fact that much of a patient's last year of treatment was useless or harmful. But the retrospective knowledge that low-value care is common at life's end does not typically get translated into an effective, evidence-based strategy for changing treatment and spending patterns near the end of life, for a variety of reasons. For instance, a multifaceted inertia favors the systematic, aggressive provision of care, much of which is understood in retrospect to have provided little benefit.

Standing in the way of reduced low-value health spending are existing systemwide financial incentives that favor delivering more treatment—incentives that align well with the professional ethos in American medicine that more is better. (In Rosenbaum's essay,[15] she suggested that professional norms and a desire for certainty—which can prompt excessive testing and multiple follow-up procedures—may actually be more influential than financial gain in driving the delivery of much care that is later recognized to have been of low value.) The United States' complex incentive structure did not form in a vacuum, and it is not surprising that health care providers in a culture that uses military metaphors for health problems ("We will wage a war on cancer"; "She lost her fight") assume that patients and their families want all illnesses treated aggressively.

The behavioral economics and social psychology literatures have detailed factors that interfere with individuals' ability to make more cost-effective end-of-life health care decisions, particularly well-known behavioral biases that limit people's ability to make rational decisions. First, when there is a possibility, however slight, of a miracle recovery, hope springs eternal. According to prospect theory,[17,18] people tend to overweight low-probability events (which explains why they pay a premium for both lottery tickets and expensive insurance coverage), and they do so especially in emotionally charged situations, such as when they are judging the potential for recovery from an illness that has been deemed terminal.[19]

Second, people tend to give undue weight to outcomes in the very near term, such as the possibility of keeping a loved one alive just a little bit longer, and to drastically discount future outcomes. They tend, for instance, to undervalue the years of financial misery that may result from this decision or the regret that they may feel about the poor quality of life a loved one experienced during their weeks, months, or years of extended life.[20] Third, most people find even thinking about sacrificing life out of financial concern terribly unpleasant—people tend to avoid even contemplating making trade-offs between sacred values, such as human life, and secular values, such as money, when the decision involves a particular individual who is "infinitely important."[21]

A Strategy for Moving Away From Low-Value Care

As I noted earlier, allowing Medicare patients who are well-informed about their care options to refuse last-ditch medical care in return for reimbursement of medical and social services not currently covered by the Medicare program's benefit package could improve the value that patients and their families receive from Medicare spending. The new services might include, for instance, flexible home-based social care that helps patients deal with limitations in dressing, bathing, eating, and other activities of daily living. More radical options could also be imagined, such as giving cash to patients who forgo care that is understood to be of low value; the money can then be used for whatever purpose they choose. Right now, hospice care is limited to cases in which physicians certify that a patient is likely to die within six months; such limitations could be relaxed, allowing patients to choose to receive palliative care earlier in their disease course, without first having to cease curative care.

Before instituting specific plans along these lines, Medicare will need to perform careful pilot tests, and monitoring will be essential to ensure that patients and family caregivers understand the options offered and the choices they make. But a study called CHAT (Choosing Health Plans All Together) that I conducted at Duke University with several colleagues already supports the notion that patients would appreciate adjustments in what Medicare will cover and that seriously ill patients are able to engage in difficult trade-offs, especially when they are able to talk about them with other patients. We found evidence[22] that Medicare beneficiaries with advanced cancer and their family members or other caregivers would be willing to forgo last-ditch cancer treatments that are often judged retrospectively to be of low value in return for having the flexibility to receive "high-touch, low-tech" care designed to improve quality of life. In the cancer setting, last-ditch care typically means experimental chemotherapy, whereas high-touch, low-tech care could take the form of hospice-like services or social care such as a nurse's aide who can help an elderly person with activities of daily living instead of a long-shot bid for a miracle cure.

The CHAT study provided theoretical choices to patient participants,[22] who were essentially given a budget and asked to select multiple care options from a list of 15 benefit categories, including three options that Medicare did not cover: visits by a nurse's aide for a few hours each day to help with basic tasks like using the toilet, dressing, or cooking (perhaps to allow an adult child to have a break); *concurrent palliative care*, which involves hospice-like services that

25%
Medicare dollars spent during the last year of a beneficiary's life

9%
Six-month survival rate in patients diagnosed with platinum-resistant ovarian cancer

38
Percentage point drop in adult smokers since 1950

"Medicare's home hospice coverage provides a nursing visit only every two to three days, even though the patient's care needs are often much greater"

a patient can receive before deciding to cease curative care (a decision currently required for hospice care to begin); and cash that could be used for anything, including such nonmedical purposes as paying for rent or food. More than 40% of participants chose to allocate some of their budget to one or more of the services that the Medicare benefit package does not now cover, which reduced the amount of traditional medical care they could receive.

Although the patients knew that the study was hypothetical and their answers did not affect the care they were allowed to receive later, the results indicate that patients and families would not only be willing to exert more choice and take more responsibility when allocating their Medicare benefits, but they would also do so in ways that could improve satisfaction with end-of-life care and potentially reduce the cost of the care they choose to receive. The tendency of participants to allocate Medicare resources away from last-ditch, low-value care and toward other care suggests, as well, that more freedom of choice could improve health equity by allowing individuals who have different preferences because of disparities (such as difficulty affording transportation to doctors' offices or not having a family member who can afford to miss work to help them out) to improve the value of their medical spending by choosing the services most important to them.

Three Guiding Principles for Experimentation in Medicare

The CHAT study[22] provided important evidence that patients might choose different care paths if they had the option, but Medicare (via the Centers for Medicare and Medicaid Innovation or a similar governmental office) needs to test the merits of different options and examine whether patients will stick with expressed preferences when making actual care decisions. It also needs to determine if such coverage changes are acceptable from policy, financial, and ethical perspectives and to identify their impact (if any) on the cost of care that patients receive. Applying the principles that follow should help to ensure that the outcomes of these proposed studies are translated into policy changes that better meet the needs of patients and reduce disparities in the care given to disadvantaged groups.

Principle 1: In each demonstration study, select a condition that frequently results in provision of low-value care at the end of life and offer options that are more flexible than those Medicare now provides. One condition that could be considered for such a study is platinum-resistant ovarian cancer in patients who have been hospitalized. Such patients have a 9% chance of surviving for six months, with none surviving 12 months.[23] These patients are usually offered a choice between third- or fourth-line chemotherapy and hospice care. Many patients and families who opt for home-based (instead of institutional) hospice care are surprised to discover that Medicare's home hospice coverage provides a nursing visit only every two to three days, even though the patient's care needs are often much greater.

A pilot study could offer patients in this situation a choice between last-ditch medical treatment or a lump sum to be used as desired, such as by paying for home-based care to help with tasks such as bathing, dressing, and cooking, which is not currently covered by the Medicare benefit package. The traditional hospice benefit would remain, and the new benefit might be thought of as "hospice plus." If pilot studies provide evidence that this approach can work, then similar studies could be developed for very common conditions, such as congestive heart failure,[24] in which the length of survival is less clear than in the ovarian cancer example and patients are likely to make longer use of the high-touch, low-tech option if it is selected. Medicare could design studies so that they evaluate the degree to which health equity is addressed by the decisions patients make.

I am talking here about the types of pilot tests that should be undertaken to improve the match between covered services and patient needs, but policymakers are sure to also consider the results from a financial perspective. If the goal is improving health equity, shifting funding from low- to high-value care would be enough to achieve such a goal, and saving money would not be a key consideration. If saving money for Medicare were a key aspect of pilot tests, then the structure of the test would likely be different. Either type of test is reasonable, but the goals of a test should be made clear to patients and families, who will have to be meaningfully involved in the allocation decisions that are an inherent part of such pilot tests. For example, if a low-income Medicare beneficiary chooses home-based care in lieu of expensive last-ditch chemotherapy, that decision would likely reduce Medicare's overall costs for this person's care. If, on the basis of the individual's low income, the person was also granted cash to pay bills and reduce family strain, this provision would reduce the cost savings to Medicare but could improve health equity.

Principle 2: Commit to an evidence-based process. Rosenbaum[15] has noted that the less-is-more crusade is backed more by belief than by evidence, and I agree that a full commitment to evidence is required if an attempt to shift from low-value spending to high-value spending is to be made. The outcomes of all participants—patients, families, and providers—need to be measured and recorded, along with the effects on Medicare's finances. As the evidence base accumulates over time, the information provided to patients, families, and providers (who will have to communicate these options to patients) should be updated. New treatment options—such as a new drug that is clearly beneficial for late-stage ovarian cancer—would have to be taken into account, and a pilot test might even have to be stopped in such a case, much as a clinical trial of a new drug is often stopped if the early results are convincing. Ever-improving information, collected while following patients from choices to outcomes, is the only way to solve the two-sided learning problem—ensuring that that the insights gained by families and by providers get captured and used instead of going nowhere.

Principle 3: Adopt an ethic of harm reduction. The goal of reducing low-value care should be viewed through a lens of harm reduction, or the acceptance that some negative outcomes or behaviors will not be eradicated but can be reduced. Requiring new Medicare policies to instantly eliminate all mismatches between patients' needs and their care would be unrealistic; small gains and improvements are victories and should be valued for the reduction in suffering they facilitate.

The evolution of smoking policies in the United States offers an example of the value of focusing persistently on harm reduction. In 1950, 55% of the adult population smoked, and the current rate of 18% was unimaginable. The transition took 75 years of multifaceted policy efforts, combined with shifting cultural norms that were influenced by policy changes but also enabled the changes to be enacted.[25-27] Policymakers need to adopt a long time horizon to judge success. Today, many Americans find it hard to believe that airlines still allowed smoking on planes in 1994, yet people in 1975 would have found it hard to believe that the practice would ever end.

A reduction in low-value care for one condition, such as platinum-resistant ovarian cancer, would have only a small impact on the Medicare program as a whole. However, it could be the beginning of a sustained effort that could have a large impact over time as the general idea is applied to more common conditions.

Following Through

Using these guiding principles, Medicare could design and test a series of pilot studies in which patients and families could decline care that evidence suggested was often of low value and select benefits that are not currently covered by Medicare, such as long-term support for caring for the elderly at home, hospice-like services that focus on symptom relief and maximizing the quality of life before a patient becomes eligible for hospice, and even cash that could be used for any purpose chosen by the patient. Such pilot studies could provide insight into whether and how patients and families are able to make use of existing clinical evidence relating to the prognoses associated with the treatments available for the patients' condition. The findings would then be used to help patients and family members overcome their lack of knowledge due to the two-sided learning problem by providing them with information about the experiences of other patients. The collected results could potentially lead to changes in the benefits that the Medicare program agrees to cover.

Congress and officials in the executive branch responsible for determining what Medicare covers and the public (which both uses and pays for Medicare) would need to keep the following questions in mind when considering whether to adjust coverage rules in response to the findings of pilot studies:

- What are the differences in survival and quality of life in patients given the most common treatments?

- What are the costs of these different options, to Medicare and to patients and their families?

- Of the common treatments, are any more expensive and less effective than others? Should coverage be eliminated for the least effective approaches? (Such decisions would be controversial if implemented via a top-down administrative process, but they may be accepted by providers, patients, and families if they are driven by the results of pilot studies in which patients make the decisions.)

- How can new evidence on patient and family satisfaction with different kinds of coverage options tested in pilot studies be used to ensure that the menu of benefits made available by Medicare to patients remains up to date with the options patients and families currently desire?

- How can the way the health care system obtains information about patient and family preferences be improved?

- Can the communication of uncertainty to patients and families be improved?

Of course, it is one thing to offer patients a high-value home-care option through Medicare; it is another thing to get patients to choose this high-value option. An abundance of behavioral research suggests that the way in which options are presented to patients and their families (that is, the *choice architecture*) can critically influence their decisions.[28,29] The optimal choice architecture must be carefully designed and tested, but behavioral research provides some educated guesses about which approaches might work best.

First, research suggests that policymakers should be careful to avoid any language that suggests a trade-off between the patient's life expectancy and money, focusing instead on improving the well-being of the patient. Second, numerous studies have found that defaults have an outsized impact on choices.[30] Thus, a poor prognosis by a clinician might trigger a protocol in which Medicare presents the home care option as the default choice from which patients must opt out to receive continued low-value treatment. This presentation may convey an implicit endorsement of home care and lead patients to construe home support, palliative care, and additional financial support as something they would have to give up to obtain low-value treatment,[31] thereby making the home care option more attractive. Third, a home care default could be bolstered by an explanation that the default was set because of high satisfaction scores among families who have chosen it, as compared with the satisfaction scores of familes who have chose low-value hospital treatments; research suggests that when people face difficult choices, they can be swayed by the preferences of others who faced a similar choice.[32]

Implications for Health Equity

The possibility that the pilot study research program I have described could identify low-value spending in a health insurance program open to everyone age 65 years and older means that resources could be freed for reallocation to high-value spending, which could, in turn, improve health equity. For instance, funding could be steered to benefits more useful to disadvantaged groups, such as cash; home-based long-term care that is not currently covered by Medicare; or home modifications, such as ramps, walk-in showers, and the like, that would allow people to stay at home in spite of illness. Of course, Medicare officials and Congress, which approves the Medicare budget, would have to choose to reallocate spending in a way that would invest resources in options that are not currently covered in Medicare's benefit package, instead of using the savings to reduce the size of Medicare's overall budget.

The CHAT study conducted in North Carolina gives an indication of how evidence-based revisions to Medicare offerings could improve health equity. Recall that the CHAT protocol hypothetically offered three types of benefits that Medicare does not cover. Nearly one in five participants reallocated at least some of their finite spending money to all three types of benefits (home-based long-term care, concurrent palliative care, and cash that could be used for any purpose); 40% choose at least one. The most important predictor was race: Black participants were nearly twice as likely as Whites (odds ratio = 1.91, 95% confidence interval [1.14, 3.23]; see note A) to consistently allocate resources to those options. Race was the only statistically significant predictor of choosing all three noncovered benefits, after controlling for age, gender, income, marital status, health status, and out-of-pocket spending. This finding suggests that some people who typically face health disparities (such as less access to care and worse health outcomes) may be more interested in choosing to receive some of their Medicare entitlement through the types of benefits that they anticipate would be of higher value to them when they are facing an end-of-life situation. Although the exercise[22] described was theoretical, all the study participants had cancer, so the experimental situation was not implausible.

A reduction in Medicare costs could even have an indirect impact on health equity if

"funding could be steered to benefits more useful to disadvantaged groups, such as cash"

the government decided to respond to such a change by lowering (or at least not increasing) the amount that younger generations pay in payroll and income taxes to finance Medicare today for elderly beneficiaries. Easing the financing burden on workers would disproportionately help low-income workers, which should increase health equity, given the correlation between income and health.

In research seminars, when I discuss the general idea of altering Medicare in ways that would improve end-of-life care, people often invoke a study called SUPPORT[33] as an argument against it. They say that the approach has been tried and failed—in the sense that, although SUPPORT documented problems with aggressive care near the end of life, the information did not change patient and family preferences or the care people received.

The criticism that the approach has been tried unsuccessfully is wrong for two reasons. First, the SUPPORT study[33] targeted patient and family decisionmaking in the intensive care unit. When a patient arrives in the intensive care unit, it is too late for well-reasoned and nuanced decisionmaking; at that point, patients are already a part of a system set up to do everything by default. Care decisions need to be made far upstream. Second, SUPPORT is more than two decades old, and the baby boomers who are flooding into Medicare differ culturally from their parents: they are more likely to want to direct more of their care, an inclination that could be harnessed in the way I have suggested.

I also respond to doubt by noting that the persistence of health inequity and Medicare's financial problems mean that out-of-the-box changes need to be considered and discussed.

If patients and families who are given evidence-based information decide to take advantage of new high-value care options, this outcome provides some evidence that patients and families may be willing to consider more radical changes to what benefits are provided by Medicare, so long as patients maintain control over their choice of benefits.

A Brighter Future

The United States needs to engage in a broad discussion about the care its citizens receive as they age and endure illness and disability. Children, grandchildren, and great-grandchildren foot the bill as their elders join the Medicare program. Because the only thing that everyone will inevitably do is die, health researchers and policymakers urgently need to solve the two-sided learning problem, which keeps patients' and providers' insights into the flaws of today's end-of-life treatments from being translated into care that matches patients' needs. Solving the problem could provide large benefits to each of us as individuals and to society as a whole and help to transform the health care system into one that learns.[34] Such a system would provide a more just and equitable distribution of spending in the Medicare program and, in so doing, could spur broader reconsiderations of spending across the life course.

author affiliation

Taylor: Duke University. Corresponding author's e-mail: don.taylor@duke.edu.

author note

The author thanks Lisa Rosenbaum and Amitabh Chandra for comments on earlier drafts. Errors and conclusions are the authors responsibility.

endnote

A. Editors' note to nonscientists: An odds ratio conveys how the presence of one factor increases the odds of having a second factor present. In this case, an odds ratio of 1.91 means that the odds of reallocating resources were almost twice as likely for Blacks as for Whites. The 95% confidence interval indicates that there is less than a 5% probability that the odds ratio would fall outside the range of 1.14–3.23. In other words, if you took 20 samples from this population, you would expect that 19 out of 20 times, the odds ratio would be higher than 1.14 and lower than 3.23.

references

1. Braveman, P., Arkin, E., Orleans, T., Proctor, D., & Plough, A. (2017). *What is health equity? And what difference does a definition make?* Princeton, NJ: Robert Wood Johnson Foundation.

2. Woolf, S. H., & Aron, L. (Eds.). (2013). *U.S. health in international perspective: Shorter lives, poorer health.* Washington, DC: National Academies Press.

3. Bradley, E. H., & Taylor, L. A. (2013). *The American health care paradox: Why spending more is getting us less.* Washington, DC: Public Affairs.

4. Williams, D. R., McClellan, M. B., & Rivlin, A. M. (2010). Beyond the Affordable Care Act: Achieving real improvements in Americans' health. *Health Affairs, 29,* 1481–1488.

5. McGinnis, J. M., Williams-Russo, P., & Knickman, J. R. (2002). The case for more active policy attention to health promotion. *Health Affairs, 21,* 78–93.

6. Smedley, B. D., & Syme, S. L. (2000). *Promoting health: Intervention strategies from social and behavioral research.* Washington, DC: National Academies Press.

7. Cutler, D. M., & Lleras-Muney, A. (2006). *Education and health: Evaluating theories and evidence* (NBER Working Paper No. 12352). Cambridge, MA: National Bureau of Economic Research.

8. Schoeni, R. F., House, J. S., Kaplan, G. A., & Pollack, H. (Eds.). (2010). *Making Americans healthier: Social and economic policy as health policy.* New York, NY: Russell Sage Foundation.

9. Riley, G. F., & Lubitz, J. D. (2010). Long-term trends in Medicare payments in the last year of life. *Health Services Research, 45,* 565–576.

10. Colla, C. H., Morden, N. E., Sequist, T. D., Schpero, W. L., & Rosenthal, M. B. (2015). Choosing wisely: Prevalence and correlates of low-value health care services in the United States. *Journal of General Internal Medicine, 30,* 221–228.

11. Rosenberg, A., Agiro, A., Gottlieb, M., Barron, J., Brady, P., Liu, Y., Li, C., & DeVries, A. (2015). Early trends among seven recommendations from the Choosing Wisely campaign. *JAMA Internal Medicine, 175,* 1913–1920.

12. Petrinec, A. B., & Daly, B. J. (2016). Post-traumatic stress symptoms in post-ICU family members: Review and methodological challenges. *Western Journal of Nursing Research, 38,* 57–78.

13. Kross, E. K., Engelberg, R. A., Gries, C. J., Nielsen, E. L., Zatzick, D., & Curtis, J. (2011). ICU care associated with symptoms of depression and posttraumatic stress disorder among family members of patients who die in the ICU. *Chest, 139,* 795–801.

14. Siegel, M. D., Hayes, E., Vanderwerker, L. C., Loseth, D. B., & Prigerson, H. G. (2008). Psychiatric illness in the next of kin of patients who die in the intensive care unit. *Critical Care Medicine, 36,* 1722–1728.

15. Rosenbaum, L. (2017). The less-is-more crusade—Are we overmedicalizing or oversimplifying? *New England Journal of Medicine, 377,* 2392–2397.

16. Einav, L., Finkelstein, A., Mullainathan, S., & Obermeyer, Z. (2018, June 29). Predictive modeling of U.S. health care spending in late life. *Science, 360,* 1462–1465.

17. Kahneman, D., & Tversky, A. (1979). Prospect theory: An analysis of decision under risk. *Econometrica, 47,* 263–291.

18. Tversky, A., & Kahneman, D. (1992). Advances in prospect theory: Cumulative representation of uncertainty. *Journal of Risk and Uncertainty, 5,* 297–323.

19. Rottenstreich, Y., & Hsee, C. K. (2001). Money, kisses, and electric shocks: On the affective psychology of risk. *Psychological Science, 12,* 185–190.

20. Frederick, S., Loewenstein, G., & O'Donoghue, T. (2002). Time discounting and time preference: A critical review. *Journal of Economic Literature, 40,* 351–401.

21. Tetlock, P. E., Kristel, O. V., Elso, S. B., Lerner, J. S., & Green, M. C. (2000). The psychology of the unthinkable: Taboo trade-offs, forbidden base rates, and heretical counterfactuals. *Journal of Personality and Social Psychology, 78,* 853–870.

22. Taylor, D. H., Jr., Danis, M., Zafar, S. Y., Howie, L. J., Samsa, G. P., Wolf, S. P., & Abernethy, A. P. (2014). There is a mismatch between the Medicare benefit package and the preferences of patients with cancer and their caregivers. *Journal of Clinical Oncology, 32,* 3163–3168.

23. Foote, J., Lopez-Acevedo, M., Samsa, G., Lee, P. S., Kamal, A. H., Secord, A. A., & Havrilesky, L. J. (2018). Predicting 6- and 12-month mortality in patients with platinum-resistant advanced stage ovarian cancer: Prognostic model to guide palliative care referrals. *International Journal of Gynecological Cancer, 28,* 302–307.

24. Downar, J., Goldman, R., Pinto, R., Englesakis, M., & Adhikari, N. K. J. (2017). The "surprise question" for predicting death in seriously ill patients: A systematic review and meta-analysis. *CMAJ, 189,* E484–E493.

25. Sloan, F. A., Ostermann, J., Picone, G., Conover, C., & Taylor, D. H., Jr. (2004). *The price of smoking.* Cambridge, MA: MIT Press.

26. Sloan, F. A., Smith, V. K., & Taylor, D. H., Jr. (2003). *The smoking puzzle: Information, risk perception, and choice.* Cambridge, MA: Harvard University Press.

27. Sloan, F. A., Smith, V. K., & Taylor, D. H., Jr. (2002). Information, addiction, and "bad choices": Lessons from a century of cigarettes. *Economic Letters, 77,* 147–155.

28. Thaler, R. H., & Sunstein, C. R. (2008). *Nudge: Improving decisions about health, wealth, and happiness.* New Haven, CT: Yale University Press.

29. Johnson, E., Shu, S. B., Dellaert, B. G. C., Fox, C. R., Goldstein, D. G., Haubl, G., & Larrick, R. P. (2012). Beyond nudges: Tools of a choice architecture. *Marketing Letters, 23,* 487–504.

30. Johnson, E. J., & Goldstein, D. (2003, November 21). Do defaults save lives? *Science, 302,* 1338–1339.

31. Dinner, I., Johnson, E. J., Goldstein, D. G., & Liu, K. (2011). Partitioning default effects: Why people choose not to choose. *Journal of Experimental Psychology: Applied, 17,* 332–341.

32. Cialdini, R. B. (2009). *Influence: Science and practice* (5th ed.). Boston, MA: Allyn & Bacon.

33. The Writing Group for the SUPPORT Investigators. (1995). A controlled trial to improve care for seriously ill hospitalized patients: The Study to Understand Prognoses and Preferences for Outcomes and Risks of Treatments (SUPPORT). *JAMA, 274,* 1591–1598.

34. Committee on the Learning Health Care System in America & Smith, M., Saunders, R., Stuckhardt, L., & McGinnis, M. (Eds.). (2013). *Best care at lower cost: The path to continuously learning health care in America.* Washington, DC: National Academies Press.

editorial policy

Behavioral Science & Policy (BSP) is an international, peer-reviewed publication of the Behavioral Science & Policy Association and Brookings Institution Press. BSP features short, accessible articles describing actionable policy applications of behavioral scientific research that serves the public interest. Articles submitted to BSP undergo a dual-review process: For each article, leading disciplinary scholars review for scientific rigor and experts in relevant policy areas review for practicality and feasibility of implementation. Manuscripts that pass this dual-review are edited to ensure their accessibility to policy makers, scientists, and lay readers. BSP is not limited to a particular point of view or political ideology.

Manuscripts can be submitted in a number of different formats, each of which must clearly explain specific implications for public- and/or private-sector policy and practice.

External review of the manuscript entails evaluation by at least two outside referees—at least one in the policy arena and at least one in the disciplinary field.

Professional editors trained in BSP's style work with authors to enhance the accessibility and appeal of the material for a general audience.

Each of the sections below provides general information for authors about the manuscript submission process. We recommend that you take the time to read each section and review carefully the BSP Editorial Policy before submitting your manuscript to *Behavioral Science & Policy*.

Manuscript Categories

Manuscripts can be submitted in a number of different categories, each of which must clearly demonstrate the empirical basis for the article as well as explain specific implications for (public and/or private-sector) policy and practice:

- Proposals ($\leq$ 2,500 words) specify scientifically grounded policy proposals and provide supporting evidence including concise reports of relevant studies. This category is most appropriate for describing new policy implications of previously published work or a novel policy recommendation that is supported by previously published studies.
- Reports ($\leq$ 3000 words) provide a summary of output and actionable prescriptions that emerge from a workshop, working group, or standing organization in the behavioral policy space. In some cases such papers may consist of summaries of a much larger published report that also includes some novel material such as meta-analysis, actionable implications, process lessons, reference to related work by others, and/or new results not presented in the initial report. These papers are not merely summaries of a published report, but also should provide substantive illustrations of the research or recommendations and insights about the implications of the report content or process for others proposing to do similar work. Submitted papers will undergo BSP review for rigor and accessibility that is expedited to facilitate timely promulgation.
- Findings ($\leq$ 4,000 words) report on results of new studies and/or substantially new analysis of previously reported data sets (including formal meta-analysis) and the policy implications of the research findings. This category is most appropriate for presenting new evidence that supports a particular policy recommendation. The additional length of this format is designed to accommodate a summary of methods, results, and/or analysis of studies (though some finer details may be relegated to supplementary online materials).
- Reviews ($\leq$ 5,000 words) survey and synthesize the key findings and policy implications of research in a specific disciplinary area or on a specific policy topic. This could take the form of describing a general-purpose behavioral tool for policy makers or a set of behaviorally grounded insights for addressing a particular policy challenge.
- Other Published Materials. BSP will sometimes solicit or accept *Essays* ($\leq$ 5,000 words) that present a unique perspective on behavioral policy; *Letters* ($\leq$ 500 words) that provide a forum for responses from readers and contributors, including policy makers and public figures; and *Invitations* ($\leq$ 1,000 words with links to online Supplemental Material), which are requests from policy makers for contributions from the behavioral science community on a particular policy issue. For example, if a particular agency is facing a specific challenge and seeks input from the behavioral science community, we would welcome posting of such solicitations.

Review and Selection of Manuscripts

On submission, the manuscript author is asked to indicate the most relevant disciplinary area and policy area addressed by his/her manuscript. (In the case of some papers, a "general" policy category designation may be appropriate.) The relevant Senior Disciplinary Editor and the Senior Policy Editor provide an initial screening of the manuscripts. After initial screening, an appropriate Associate Policy Editor and Associate Disciplinary Editor serve as the stewards of each manuscript as it moves through the editorial process. The manuscript author will receive an email within approximately two weeks of submission, indicating whether the article has been sent to outside referees for further consideration. External review of the manuscript entails evaluation by at least two outside referees. In most cases, Authors will receive a response from BSP within approximately 60 days of submission. With rare exception, we will submit manuscripts to no more than two rounds of full external review. We generally do not accept re-submissions of material without an explicit invitation from an editor. Professional editors trained in the BSP style will collaborate with the author of any manuscript recommended for publication to enhance the accessibility and appeal of the material to a general audience (i.e., a broad range of behavioral scientists, public- and private-sector policy makers, and educated lay public). We anticipate no more than two rounds of feedback from the professional editors.

Standards for Novelty

BSP seeks to bring new policy recommendations and/or new evidence to the attention of public and private sector policy makers that are supported by rigorous behavioral and/or social science research. Our emphasis is on novelty of the policy application and the strength of the supporting evidence for that recommendation. We encourage submission of work based on new studies, especially field studies (for Findings and Proposals) and novel syntheses of previously published work that have a strong empirical foundation (for Reviews).

BSP will also publish novel treatments of previously published studies that focus on their significant policy implications. For instance, such a paper might involve re-working of the general emphasis, motivation, discussion of implications, and/or a re-analysis of existing data to highlight policy-relevant implications or prior work that have not been detailed elsewhere.

In our checklist for authors we ask for a brief statement that explicitly details how the present work differs from previously published work (or work under review elsewhere). When in doubt, we ask that authors include with their submission copies of related papers. Note that any text, data, or figures excerpted or paraphrased from other previously published material must clearly indicate the original source with quotation and citations as appropriate.

Authorship

Authorship implies substantial participation in research and/or composition of a manuscript. All authors must agree to the order of author listing and must have read and approved submission of the final manuscript. All authors are responsible for the accuracy and integrity of the work, and the senior author is required to have examined raw data from any studies on which the paper relies that the authors have collected.

Data Publication

BSP requires authors of accepted empirical papers to submit all relevant raw data (and, where relevant, algorithms or code for analyzing those data) and stimulus materials for publication on the journal web site so that other investigators or policymakers can verify and draw on the analysis contained in the work. In some cases, these data may be redacted slightly to protect subject anonymity and/or comply with legal restrictions. In cases where a proprietary data set is owned by a third party, a waiver to this requirement may be granted. Likewise, a waiver may be granted if a dataset is particularly complex, so that it would be impractical to post it in a sufficiently annotated form (e.g. as is sometimes the case for brain imaging data). Other waivers will be considered where appropriate. Inquiries can be directed to the BSP office.

Statement of Data Collection Procedures

BSP strongly encourages submission of empirical work that is based on multiple studies and/or a meta-analysis of several datasets. In order to protect against false positive results, we ask that authors of empirical work fully disclose relevant details concerning their data collection practices (if not in the main text then in the supplemental online materials). In particular, we ask that authors report how they determined their sample size, all data exclusions (if any), all manipulations, and all measures in the studies presented. (A template for these disclosures is included in our checklist for authors, though in some cases may be most appropriate for presentation online as Supplemental Material; for more information, see Simmons, Nelson, & Simonsohn, 2011, *Psychological Science, 22, 1359–1366*).

Copyright and License

Copyright to all published articles is held jointly by the Behavioral Science & Policy Association and Brookings Institution Press, subject to use outlined in the *Behavioral Science & Policy* publication agreement (a waiver is considered only in cases where one's employer formally and explicitly prohibits work from being copyrighted; inquiries should be directed to the BSPA office). Following publication, the manuscript author may post the accepted version of the article on his/her personal web site, and may circulate the work to colleagues and students for educational and research purposes. We also allow posting in cases where funding agencies explicitly request access to published manuscripts (e.g., NIH requires posting on PubMed Central).

Open Access

BSP posts each accepted article on our website in an open access format at least until that article has been bundled into an issue. At that point, access is granted to journal subscribers and members of the Behavioral Science & Policy Association. Questions regarding institutional constraints on open access should be directed to the editorial office.

Supplemental Material

While the basic elements of study design and analysis should be described in the main text, authors are invited to submit Supplemental Material for online publication that helps elaborate on details of research methodology and analysis of their data, as well as links to related material available online elsewhere. Supplemental material should be included to the extent that it helps readers evaluate the credibility of the contribution, elaborate on the findings presented in the paper, or provide useful guidance to policy makers wishing to act on the policy recommendations advanced in the paper. This material should be presented in as concise a manner as possible.

Embargo

Authors are free to present their work at invited colloquia and scientific meetings, but should not seek media attention for their work in advance of publication, unless the reporters in question agree to comply with BSP's press embargo. Once accepted, the paper will be considered a privileged document and only be released to the press and public when published online. BSP will strive to release work as quickly as possible, and we do not anticipate that this will create undue delays.

Conflict of Interest

Authors must disclose any financial, professional, and personal relationships that might be construed as possible sources of bias.

Use of Human Subjects

All research using human subjects must have Institutional Review Board (IRB) approval, where appropriate.